הגדה של פסח

Gates of Freedom:

A Passover Haggadah

by

Chaim Stern

Visual Interpretations by

Todd Siler

Introduction by

Eugene B. Borowitz

Chappaqua, New York

Chaim Stern is rabbi of Temple Beth El of Northern Westchester and Editor of the new liturgy of Reform Judaism for the Central Conference of American Rabbis, beginning with Gates of Prayer. He is, in addition, Editor of other works of liturgy and Co-Editor of the liturgy of the British Liberal movement.

Eugene B. Borowitz is Professor of Education and Jewish Religious Thought at Hebrew Union College-Jewish Institute of Religion, author of many works on Jewish thought and life, and a leading theologian of contemporary Judaism.

Todd Siler recently received his M.S. in visual art from the Massachusetts Institute of Technology and is pursuing advanced studies at that institution. He has recently exhibited in New York, Montreal, and Paris.

Published by   Rossel Books,
                P.O. Box 87
                Chappaqua, NY 10514

Library of Congress Cataloging in Publication Data

Haggadah (Reform, Stern)
    (Hagadah shel Pesah) = Gates of freedom

    English and Hebrew
    Bibliography: p.
    1. Reform Judaism—Liturgy—Texts.   2. Haggadah (Reform,
Stern)—Texts.   3. Seder. I. Stern, Chaim. II. Siler, Todd.
III. Title. IV. Title: Gates of freedom.
BM675.P4Z667   296.4'37   81-84191
ISBN 0-940846-21-8   AACR2

Printed in the U. S. A.

Contents

v

Introduction

The Seder confounds our usual notions of "religion." It takes place at home, not in a sanctuary; is conducted by anyone or everyone, not by a rabbi; involves more eating than petitioning of God; requires us to drink more than we usually do yet isn't orgiastic; touches us with tales of a slavery we have not experienced and amazes us with Temple Rites we can hardly imagine; evokes so many family memories we can hardly think about Egypt; and gives us an opportunity for familial custom or community style that transforms a two-thousand-year-old rite into a living experience.

Some people think that great cosmic themes demand serious attention and meticulous observance. A Seder, I suppose, should have some element of high dignity running through it. But seated around the table, with family gathered from afar or, if not there, badly missed, with our annual guests and this year's invitees, I cannot help but put before me the Torah's general rule about the pilgrimage day observance, ". . . you shall rejoice in your festival." That is a command. We shall not have fulfilled our Jewish duty if we do not have a joyous time at the Seder.

How shall we do that? How shall we learn to be joyous while joining our people in their perennial service of God? In part, this *Haggadah* will help. It speaks of all the old ways in an idiom that preserves their ancient power yet addresses us who know ourselves to be as free a generation of Jews as ever lived. Again and again it suggests ways we might extend the Torah's message for this celebration deeper into our lives or further out into the world. With its many subtle interplays of tradition and modernity it lifts the spirits of all who know they must be Jews in old, familiar ways, yet somehow recreate the past in their personal fashion.

But we Jews do not believe that rites perform themselves, nor that their sacred power is unleashed merely in the doing. And surely this is true of the command to rejoice. Our contribution to this elegant text must be the creation of delight. One cannot give rules for being happy, which may be why the Rabbis limited their instructions about rejoicing. Having given us this incomparable context in which to fulfill our duty, they left the personal side largely to us. For me, elation has to do with smiling, with exchanging glances, with an occasional spontaneous comment about the text or the company, with loving what we are doing this evening and communicating that to everyone.

The real test of the evening's festivity, I suggest, lies less in being able to add to its pleasures than in overcoming its difficulties. What bothers you the most—long Hebrew passages? dry political interpolations about true

freedom? relatives who repeat the same tiresome stories? matzah balls that come out too soft or too hard? people who can't stay on tune or don't like your favorite? They too are part of Jewish celebrating. Consider them, if you can, a challenge to your Jewish spirit and see if on this holiday you can find a way to sanctify what annoys you.

My model in all this is the great unwritten but perennially observed folk rite of the Seder: knocking over a glass of wine (perhaps breaking a beautiful crystal goblet in the process). Rarely does a tablecloth go unscathed through a Seder at our house—and we are lucky if our *Haggadot* and clothing escape the miniature deluge. I have long since given up the possibility that we could make this the Seder's equivalent of breaking a glass at a wedding; could we, then, work out ways of making it unlikely that wine would ever be spilled? Probably we could, but why bother? A little spilling and a stain or two are hardly enough to dampen our joy at not being slaves. And by now, we have gotten so used to them, that we consider them a part of the festivities. This too helps constitute that wonderful web which Judaism teaches us to weave, in order to integrate the ordinary and the metaphysical. Not every spill can become a part of our rejoicing; but knowing which ones are worth our seriousness is part of what each Seder and Judaism as a whole wish to teach us.

May you celebrate in high, human, holy joy.

Eugene B. Borowitz

Preface

Pesach

In the beginnings (1500–1200 B.C.E.) there were *two* Festivals: *Pesach*, a shepherds' holiday celebrating the lambing season, and *Chag Hamatzot*, a farmers' holiday celebrating the year's first grain harvest. And still the names are preserved: Passover, the Festival of Unleavened Bread.

In the second half of the thirteenth century Israel left Egypt, and thereafter the two celebrations became a single Festival with new meanings. *Pesach* came to be understood as referring to the last of the Ten Plagues, when God 'passed over' (*pasach* = Passover) the houses of the Israelites, and the unleavened bread came to recall the haste of Israel's departure, when there was no time for bread to rise. This single Festival became *Z'man Cherutenu*, 'The Season of our Freedom', commemorating Israel's deliverance from Egyptian bondage—a deliverance seen as the supreme paradigm of the divine redemptive power in human history. In Heine's words: "Since the Exodus, Freedom has always spoken with a Hebrew accent."

Passover, then, has four aspects. It is seasonal, a rejoicing in the annual re-awakening of nature at springtime. It is historical, marking the 'birthday' of the Jewish people. It is a festival of freedom. It is a ritual of preparation for an ultimate redemption, of which our first redemption was a hint and a promise.

The Seder

From very early times Pesach has been an occasion for public worship. It also gave rise to a more intimate celebration by families or groups of families. This took place, in ancient times, at a festival meal in which the paschal lamb was eaten together with bitter herbs and unleavened bread. After the destruction of the Temple in 70 C.E., the sacrificial system came to an end, and so the lamb—a sacrifice—was omitted, but the meal continued and attained even greater importance. It also became more elaborate. To the unleavened bread and bitter herbs, other dishes were added and invested with symbolic significance.

Closely associated with the meal is the duty of parents to teach their children about the Exodus, so that each generation of Jews relives that great experience and understands its meaning. So the Bible commands: "Tell your child on that day" (Exodus 13.8). In time that command led to

the creation of a well-defined ritual known as *Seder Haggadah*, "The Order of Narration." Later Ashkenazi (European) Jews came to use the term *Seder* for the ritual as a whole, including the meal, and the term *Haggadah* for the book itself, the telling of the Exodus story along with appropriate prayers and songs.

The Haggadah

The *Haggadah* as a book dates from the ninth century, when it was included in Jewish prayerbooks and law-codes. By the twelfth century it began to be published on its own. During the long centuries before its compilation as a book, the *Haggadah* was transmitted by word of mouth, a fluid text whose core was fixed but whose details varied from time to time, and from community to community.

The publication of the *Haggadah* as a volume in its own right resulted in the production of countless manuscript editions, of which a few have survived. Some of them are richly illuminated and illustrated. They are among the masterpieces of Jewish religious art.

Since the invention of printing in the fifteenth century, something like 3,000 printed editions have appeared. Essentially the same, they nevertheless show many variations according to local custom, while the emergence of Reform Judaism in the nineteenth century heralded a period of further diversification. Even Israeli Kibbutzim (some of them anti-religious) have produced their own versions of the ancient ritual. Of making many *Haggadot* there is no end!

This Haggadah

The aim of this Haggadah is to let the traditional text speak for itself, both in its original tongue and through a new translation, with only minor omissions, abridgements, and rearrangements. In addition, we aim to sharpen its significance for the modern Jew by the inclusion of supplementary passages, some drawn from Biblical and Rabbinic Literature, some from general literature, and some newly written. This Haggadah is offered in the hope that it will help those who use it to find renewed delight in the Seder, as they experience both familiar and unfamiliar levels of meaning, relevance, and inspiration.

Preparation

Hospitality

Early in the Seder we say: "Let all who are hungry come and eat; let all who are in need come share our Passover." As an expression of this hospitality, it has long been customary to invite one or more guests. It is especially commendable to invite persons whose circumstances might otherwise prevent them from participating in a family Seder.

The Ritual

The person leading the Seder should study the Haggadah in advance and plan how it is to be used (leaving some room for spontaneity). Thus, some passages may be recited in English. Some may be spoken and others sung. Moreover, the Seder may be shortened by omitting some of the passages, or lengthened by supplementary readings from appropriate anthologies or by additional explanations and discussion. For the latter purpose, the *Notes* at the end of this volume should prove useful. They also give the sources of all passages.

The Meal

There is no standard or stipulated menu for the Seder meal, which is a matter of regional and family tradition, but the following are needed for the symbolic role they play in the Seder (their significance will be explained in the text):

1. WINE, red or white, in sufficient quantity to enable each participant's glass to be filled four times.
2. KARPAS, Green Herbs such as parsley, lettuce, chicory, celery, or any other green salad vegetable; a small quantity for each participant.
3. SALT WATER, in which the Green Herbs (KARPAS) will be dipped by each participant.
4. MATZAH, Unleavened Bread made from any one of the five species of grain, usually wheat, by a process which ensures that the flour is kept perfectly dry throughout.

5. ZEROA, a roasted shank-bone with some meat on it, reminiscent of the paschal lamb. (Therefore, some use a lamb bone; others use a beef or even a chicken bone.) As it is only for display, one is sufficient.

6. BEITSAH, an egg boiled, or first boiled and then roasted, in its shell. This too is only for display.

7. MAROR, Bitter Herbs, a small quantity for each participant. Though some use the leaves, stem, or main root of lettuce (CHAZERET), the most common practice is to use sliced or grated root of horseradish.

8. CHAROSET, a sweet paste in which the Maror is dipped, so that each participant will require a small quantity. Recipes vary but usually include (a) chopped or grated nuts; (b) chopped or grated apples or other fruit (especially those mentioned in the *Song of Songs*); (c) a little wine; (d) cinnamon or ginger. The latter (if used) should preferably be sliced into thin sticks, rather than grated, to symbolize the straw, as the rest symbolizes the clay, with which the Israelites were forced to make bricks in Egypt.

The Table

The Seder table should be given a festive appearance, with a white table-cloth and the best dishes and silver. The seasonal aspect of Pesach makes it appropriate to decorate the table with spring flowers. A candlestick holding two candles (more are permissible) should be placed in front of the person who is to kindle the lights.

In some communities there is a tradition—for which there is no very cogent reason but which may be felt to lend an extra touch of solemnity to the occasion—that the person who conducts the Seder wears a white robe called *Kittel*. At certain points in the Seder, there is an old custom of 'leaning' to the left; to facilitate this, the leader at least should be provided with a cushion: which serves also to remind us of the leisure, the ease our forebears did not enjoy in many lands of bondage.

Every participant should be provided with a Haggadah, a wine-glass, a plate containing Karpas, Matzah, Maror and Charoset, and a bowl of salt water. In recent times, it has become customary to lay an extra place, or to keep an extra chair, as a reminder of those Jews who, living under an oppressive regime, are unable to celebrate the Seder in the traditional manner.

In front of the leader there should be: (1) a Seder plate or dish (*k'arah*) for the display of Karpas, Charoset, Maror, Beitsah and Zeroa; (2) a Matzah cover in the form of a napkin with three compartments, each containing one Matzah (Seder plates and Matzah covers are obtainable at

synagogue Judaica shops or Jewish bookshops); (3) a extra glass or (preferably) silver goblet known as 'The Cup of Elijah'.

There are two customs concerning the Afikoman that should be kept in mind: (a) in many households the Afikoman is hidden by the leader; later on, the children are encouraged to look for it; (b) in other households, the *children* are encouraged to hide the Afikoman, and the *leader* must later find it. Both customs depend on the fact that the Seder meal concludes with the eating of the Afikoman, and that it cannot be completed without it. The leader should therefore bear in mind the need to have ready a prize or prizes for the child or children, with which to redeem the Afikoman.

Acknowledgments

As Editor of this Haggadah, I owe much to many. I especially thank Rabbi John D. Rayner, whose work has greatly influenced my own. Rabbi Rayner and I have collaborated in many liturgical works, from "Service of the Heart" (London, ULPS, 1967), to "A Modern Passover Haggadah" (London, ULPS, 1981, edited by Rabbi John D. Rayner with the collaboration of Rabbi Chaim Stern and with the assistance of Rabbi Julia Neuberger). I owe much that is good in the present Haggadah to him, and wish to record my gratitude.

The following read the manuscript carefully and made many helpful suggestions: Rabbi Joan B. Friedman, Rabbi Lawrence A. Hoffman, Rabbi Sandra Levine, Rabbi Michael A. Robinson, Rabbi Julius Rosenthal, of blessed memory, and Susan Stern. Cantor Kenneth Cohen's assistance in matters related to music was invaluable. Ronald Feldman helped tremendously in various ways, and especially with regard to the art. Stanley Gluck expertly advised and assisted in all aspects of this book's design. Rabbi Miles Cohen of Bet Sha'ar Press, Inc. was always helpful and patient in the typesetting and associated matters. And Seymour Rossel was always forthcoming with useful advice and information: all have my grateful thanks.

Finally, I thank the many individuals of Temple Beth El of Northern Westchester who have used this *Haggadah* in mimeographed form (and especially Myra and Milton Schubin, in whose home we have celebrated the Passover with this *Haggadah*), and whose enthusiastic response has encouraged me to offer this *Haggadah* to the community at large.

Rabbi Chaim Stern

Searching for Leaven   בדיקת חמץ

There is a custom to search for any bread or other food containing leaven by the light of a lamp or candle after dark on the eve of the day before Passover—or, if that is a Friday, the preceding evening. Some is always found, because it is secreted beforehand to provide occasion for the (two-stage) ritual. We thus fulfill the words: "You shall eat unleavened bread for seven days; moreover, on the preceding day you shall remove all leaven from your houses" (Exodus 12.15).

On the following morning, the leavened food is burned or, preferably, fed to animals or birds.

The search for leaven is called 'Bedikat Chametz', while the removal of leaven is called 'Biur Chametz'.

Before the search, the following is said:

זָכוֹר אֶת־הַיּוֹם הַזֶּה אֲשֶׁר יְצָאתֶם
מִמִּצְרַיִם, מִבֵּית עֲבָדִים; כִּי
בְּחֹזֶק יָד הוֹצִיא יְיָ אֶתְכֶם
מִזֶּה; וְלֹא יֵאָכֵל חָמֵץ.

Zachor et hayom hazeh asher y'tsatem
mimitsrayim, mibeit avadim; ki
b'chozek yad hotsi Adonai et-chem
mizeh; v'lo yei-a-cheil chameits.

Remember this day, the day you went forth from Egypt, from the house of bondage; for with a mighty hand the Eternal God led you forth to freedom; no leavened bread shall be eaten. (Exodus 13.3)

בָּרוּךְ אַתָּה יְיָ, אֱלֹהֵינוּ מֶלֶךְ
הָעוֹלָם, אֲשֶׁר קִדְּשָׁנוּ בְּמִצְוֹתָיו
וְצִוָּנוּ עַל בִּעוּר חָמֵץ.

Baruch ata Adonai, Eloheinu melech
ha-olam, asher kid'shanu b'mitsvotav
v'tsivanu al bi-ur chameits.

We praise You, Eternal God, Ruler of time and space, for You hallow us with Your Mitzvot, and call us to remove leavened bread from our homes.

After the removal of the leaven the following is recited:

הִנְנוּ מוּכָנִים לְקַבֵּל בְּבֵיתֵנוּ
אֶת־חַג הַמַּצּוֹת; יָבֹא לִקְרָאתֵנוּ
לְחֵרוּת וּלְשָׁלוֹם.

Hin'nu muchanim l'kabeil b'veiteinu
et chag hamatsot; yavo likrateinu
l'cheirut u-l'shalom.

We are now ready to welcome the Festival of Unleavened Bread into our home; may it bring us freedom and peace.

הגדה של פסח

Gates of Freedom:

A Passover Haggadah

For Leah and Pinchas,
my parents,
whose memory is a blessing,
and for
David, Philip and Michael,
my children,
whose lives are a blessing

Opening Prayer פתיחה

Leader:

Long ago, at this season, a people—*our* people—set out on a journey.

On such a night as this, Israel went forth from degradation to joy.

We give thanks for the liberations of days gone by.

And we pray for all who are still bound, still denied their human rights.

Eternal God, may all who hunger come to rejoice in a new Passover.

Let all the human family sit at Your table, drink the wine of deliverance, eat the bread of freedom:

Leader:	*All:*
freedom from bondage	and freedom from oppression,
freedom from hunger	and freedom from want,
freedom from hatred	and freedom from fear,
freedom to think	and freedom to speak,
freedom to teach	and freedom to learn,
freedom to love	and freedom to share,
freedom to hope	and freedom to rejoice,
soon, in our days,	amen.

Kindling the Lights

הדלקת הנרות

Leader:

זְכוֹר אֶת־הַיּוֹם הַזֶּה אֲשֶׁר יְצָאתֶם מִמִּצְרַיִם, מִבֵּית עֲבָדִים;
כִּי בְּחֹזֶק יָד הוֹצִיא יְיָ אֶתְכֶם מִזֶּה.

"Remember this day, the day you went forth from Egypt, from the house of bondage, for with a mighty hand Adonai, the Eternal One, led you forth to freedom."

"The people who walked in darkness have seen a great light." From bondage to freedom, from darkness to light: this has been the path of our life; for this we give thanks:

All

בָּרוּךְ אַתָּה יְיָ, אֱלֹהֵינוּ
מֶלֶךְ הָעוֹלָם, אֲשֶׁר קִדְּשָׁנוּ
בְּמִצְוֹתָיו וְצִוָּנוּ לְהַדְלִיק
נֵר שֶׁל (שַׁבָּת וְשֶׁל) יוֹם טוֹב.

Baruch ata Adonai, Eloheinu melech ha-olam, asher kid'shanu b'mitsvotav v'tsivanu l'hadlik neir shel (Shabbat v'shel) Yom Tov.

♪ p. 99

We praise You, Eternal God, Ruler of time and space, for You hallow us with Your Mitzvot, and call us to kindle the light of (Shabbat and) Yom Tov.

*   *

Leader:

For all of us, and especially for the children, who will in their turn be keepers of the flame, we ask God's blessing:

יְבָרֶכְךָ יְיָ וְיִשְׁמְרֶךָ.
יָאֵר יְיָ פָּנָיו אֵלֶיךָ וִיחֻנֶּךָּ.
יִשָּׂא יְיָ פָּנָיו אֵלֶיךָ
וְיָשֵׂם לְךָ שָׁלוֹם.

Y'varech'cha Adonai v'yishm'recha.
Ya'er Adonai panav eilecha vichuneka.
Yisa Adonai panav eilecha v'yaseim l'cha shalom.

May God bless you and keep you. May God smile upon you and be gracious to you. May God look upon you with favor and give you peace.

*   *

4

Kadesh

The cups are filled

Tonight we drink four cups of wine. There are many explanations for this custom. They represent, some have said, the 'four corners of the earth,' for freedom must reign everywhere; the four seasons of the year, for freedom must be guarded at all times; the 'four empires' that oppressed us in days of old, for tyranny must pass away as did these empires, before all the world is free. Above all, they stand for the four promises of redemption recorded in the story of the liberation of our people from Egyptian bondage: I WILL BRING YOU OUT—I WILL DELIVER YOU—I WILL REDEEM YOU—I WILL TAKE YOU TO BE MY PEOPLE (Exodus 6.6–7).

THE FIRST CUP   כוס של קדוש

Leader:

We raise our cups in remembrance of the beginning of our redemption, as it is said:

All:

אֲנִי יְיָ, וְהוֹצֵאתִי אֶתְכֶם   Ani Adonai, V'HOTSEITI et-chem
מִתַּחַת סִבְלת מִצְרָיִם.   mitachat sivlot Mitsrayim.

I am Adonai, the Eternal One, and I will BRING YOU OUT from under the Egyptian yoke.

For Shabbat

וַיְהִי־עֶרֶב וַיְהִי־בֹקֶר יוֹם הַשִּׁשִּׁי. וַיְכֻלּוּ הַשָּׁמַיִם וְהָאָרֶץ וְכָל־צְבָאָם. וַיְכַל אֱלֹהִים בַּיּוֹם הַשְּׁבִיעִי מְלַאכְתּוֹ אֲשֶׁר עָשָׂה; וַיִּשְׁבֹּת בַּיּוֹם הַשְּׁבִיעִי מִכָּל־מְלַאכְתּוֹ אֲשֶׁר עָשָׂה. וַיְבָרֶךְ אֱלֹהִים אֶת־יוֹם הַשְּׁבִיעִי וַיְקַדֵּשׁ אֹתוֹ, כִּי בוֹ שָׁבַת מִכָּל־מְלַאכְתּוֹ אֲשֶׁר־בָּרָא אֱלֹהִים לַעֲשׂוֹת.

Va-y'hi erev va-y'hi voker, yom hashishi. Va-y'chulu hashamayim v'ha-arets v'chol ts'va-am. Va-y'chal Elohim ba-yom ha-sh'vi-i m'lachto asher asa; va-yishbot ba-yom ha-sh'vi-i mikol m'lachto asher asa. Va-y'varech Elohim et yom ha-sh'vi-i va-y'kadeish oto, ki vo shavat mikol m'lachto asher bara Elohim la-asot.

6

p. 99

Leader:

בָּרוּךְ אַתָּה יְיָ, אֱלֹהֵינוּ
מֶלֶךְ הָעוֹלָם, בּוֹרֵא פְּרִי
הַגָּפֶן.

Baruch ata Adonai, Eloheinu
melech ha-olam, borei p'ri
hagafen.

We praise You, Eternal God, Ruler of time and space, Creator of
the fruit of the vine.

בָּרוּךְ אַתָּה יְיָ, אֱלֹהֵינוּ מֶלֶךְ הָעוֹלָם, אֲשֶׁר בָּחַר בָּנוּ מִכָּל־
עָם וְרוֹמְמָנוּ מִכָּל־לָשׁוֹן וְקִדְּשָׁנוּ בְּמִצְוֹתָיו. וַתִּתֶּן־לָנוּ יְיָ
אֱלֹהֵינוּ בְּאַהֲבָה   (שַׁבָּתוֹת לִמְנוּחָה וּ)מוֹעֲדִים לְשִׂמְחָה
חַגִּים וּזְמַנִּים לְשָׂשׂוֹן אֶת־יוֹם   (הַשַׁבָּת הַזֶּה וְאֶת־יוֹם)חַג
הַמַּצּוֹת הַזֶּה זְמַן חֵרוּתֵנוּ   (בְּאַהֲבָה)מִקְרָא קֹדֶשׁ זֵכֶר
לִיצִיאַת מִצְרָיִם. כִּי בָנוּ בָחַרְתָּ וְאוֹתָנוּ קִדַּשְׁתָ מִכָּל־הָעַמִּים
(וְשַׁבָּת)וּמוֹעֲדֵי קָדְשֶׁךָ   (בְּאַהֲבָה וּבְרָצוֹן)בְּשִׂמְחָה וּבְשָׂשׂוֹן
הִנְחַלְתָּנוּ. בָּרוּךְ אַתָּה יְיָ, מְקַדֵּשׁ   (הַשַׁבָּת וְ)יִשְׂרָאֵל
וְהַזְּמַנִּים.

Baruch ata Adonai, Eloheinu melech ha-olam, asher bachar
banu mikol am, v'romamanu mikol lashon, v'kid'shanu
b'mitzvotav. Vatiten lanu, Adonai Eloheinu, b'ahavah
(Shabatot lim'nucha u-) mo-adim l'simcha, chagim u-
z'manim l'sason, et yom(hashabbat hazeh v'et yom) chag
hamatzot hazeh—z'man cheruteinu, mikra kodesh, zeicher
litsi-at Mitsra-yim. Ki vanu vacharta v'otanu kidashta mikol
ha-amim,(v'shabbat) u-mo-adei kodsh'cha(b'ahava u-
v'ratson,) b'simcha u-v'sason hinchaltanu. Baruch ata
Adonai, m'kadeish(Hashabbat v') Yisra-el v'haz'manim.

We praise You, Eternal God, Ruler of time and space, for You have chosen us from all
the peoples and raised us high among the nations by hallowing us with Your Mitzvot. In
Your love, Eternal God, You have given us(Sabbaths for rest and) Festivals for gladness,
times and seasons for rejoicing: this(Shabbat and this) Feast of Pesach, the season of our
freedom, to unite in worship and recall the Exodus from Egypt. Truly, You have chosen
us from all peoples to consecrate us to Your service, and(in Your love and kindness)
have given us(Shabbat and) the Holy Festive days, a time for gladness and joy. We praise
You, Eternal One, for the holiness of(Shabbat,) the House of Israel and the Festivals.

On Saturday night, continue on p. 8

On other nights, continue on p. 9

7

Havdalah

הבדלה

On Saturday night all look at the Festival
lights and say:

All:

בָּרוּךְ אַתָּה יְיָ, אֱלֹהֵֽינוּ
מֶֽלֶךְ הָעוֹלָם, בּוֹרֵא מְאוֹרֵי
הָאֵשׁ.

Baruch ata Adonai, Eloheinu
melech ha-olam, borei m'orei
ha-eish.

We praise You, Eternal God, Ruler of time and space, Creator of the lights of fire.

Leader:

בָּרוּךְ אַתָּה יְיָ, אֱלֹהֵֽינוּ מֶֽלֶךְ הָעוֹלָם, הַמַּבְדִּיל בֵּין קֹֽדֶשׁ
לְחֹל, בֵּין אוֹר לְחֹֽשֶׁךְ, בֵּין יִשְׂרָאֵל לָעַמִּים, בֵּין יוֹם הַשְּׁבִיעִי
לְשֵֽׁשֶׁת יְמֵי הַמַּעֲשֶׂה. בֵּין קְדֻשַּׁת שַׁבָּת לִקְדֻשַּׁת יוֹם טוֹב
הִבְדַּֽלְתָּ, וְאֶת־יוֹם הַשְּׁבִיעִי מִשֵּֽׁשֶׁת יְמֵי הַמַּעֲשֶׂה קִדַּֽשְׁתָּ;
הִבְדַּֽלְתָּ וְקִדַּֽשְׁתָּ אֶת־עַמְּךָ יִשְׂרָאֵל בִּקְדֻשָּׁתֶֽךָ. בָּרוּךְ אַתָּה יְיָ,
הַמַּבְדִּיל בֵּין קֹֽדֶשׁ לְקֹֽדֶשׁ.

Baruch ata Adonai, Eloheinu melech ha-olam, hamavdil bein kodesh l'chol, bein or l'choshech, bein Yisra-el la-amim, bein yom hash'vi'i l'sheishet y'mei hama-aseh. Bein k'dushat Shabbat lik'dushat Yom Tov hivdalta, v'et yom hash'vi'i misheishet y'mei hama-aseh kidashta; hivdalta v'kidashta et am'cha Yisra-el bik'dushatecha. Baruch ata Adonai, hamavdil bein kodesh l'kodesh.

We praise You, Eternal God, Ruler of time and space, for You teach us to distinguish between holy and common, light and dark, the House of Israel and other peoples, the seventh day of rest and the six days of labor. And you have given each sacred day its own holiness, dividing Sabbath from Festival. We praise You, Eternal One, for You teach us to distinguish between the holiness of Shabbat and the holiness of Yom Tov.

8

בָּרוּךְ אַתָּה יְיָ, אֱלֹהֵינוּ Baruch ata Adonai, Eloheinu
מֶלֶךְ הָעוֹלָם, שֶׁהֶחֱיָנוּ melech ha-olam, she-hecheyanu,
וְקִיְּמָנוּ וְהִגִּיעָנוּ v'ki-y'manu, v'higi-anu
לַזְּמַן הַזֶּה. la-z'man hazeh.

We praise You, Eternal God, Ruler of time and space, for keeping us alive, for sustaining us, and for enabling us to reach this season.

All now drink the first cup

*   *

9

Karpas

כרפס

"Spring hangs her infant blossoms on the trees,
Rock'd in the cradle of the western breeze."
When earth is freed from winter's yoke,
When lambs are born and trees turn green,
We celebrate the renewal of life and growth,
of hope and love.

Rise up, my love,
my fair one, come away!
For now the winter is past,
the rains are over and gone.
The flowers appear on the earth,
the time of singing has come.
The song of the dove
is heard in our land.

קוּמִי לָךְ, רַעְיָתִי,
יָפָתִי וּלְכִי־לָךְ!
כִּי־הִנֵּה הַסְּתָו עָבָר,
הַגֶּשֶׁם חָלַף הָלַךְ לוֹ.
הַנִּצָּנִים נִרְאוּ בָאָרֶץ,
עֵת הַזָּמִיר הִגִּיעַ.
וְקוֹל הַתּוֹר
נִשְׁמַע בְּאַרְצֵנוּ.

The standing corn grows ripe,
as dew-drops bring their blessing:
food for the hungry,
healing for the sick.
The grape vines blossom,
as the heavens
yield their dew.

רְאֵה קָמָה לְמַלֹּאת
בְּרְסִיסֵי בְרָכָה:
לֶחֶם לָאוֹכֵל,
וּמַרְפֵּא וַאֲרוּכָה.
לְמַלְבִּישׁ סוּת סְמָדָר
עֲרוּמֵי שׂוֹרֵקָה;
וְהַשָּׁמַיִם יִתְּנוּ טַלָּם.

The green herbs are dipped in salt water

All:

בָּרוּךְ אַתָּה יְיָ, אֱלֹהֵינוּ
מֶלֶךְ הָעוֹלָם, בּוֹרֵא פְּרִי
הָאֲדָמָה.

Baruch ata Adonai, Eloheinu
melech ha-olam, borei p'ri
ha-adamah.

We praise You, Eternal God, Ruler of time and space, Creator of the fruit of the earth.

The green herbs are eaten

*   *

Breaking the Matzah (Yachatz)

יחץ

*GOD IS BREAD

There are people in the world so hungry that God cannot appear to them except in the form of bread. (After M. K. Gandhi)

The leader takes out the middle Matzah and breaks it in two. The larger piece, known as the 'Afikoman', will presently be hidden away either by the leader or by the children. The smaller piece is replaced between the two whole Matzot, which are raised while the following is recited:

All:

הָא לַחְמָא עַנְיָא Ha lachma anya

דִּי אֲכָלוּ אַבְהָתַנָא di achalu avahatana

בְּאַרְעָא דְמִצְרָיִם. b'ar'a d'mitzrayim.

כָּל־דִּכְפִין יֵיתֵי וְיֵכָל, kol dich-fin yeitei v'yeichul,

כָּל־דִּצְרִיךְ יֵיתֵי וְיִפְסַח. kol dits-rich yeitei v'yifsach.

הָשַׁתָּא הָכָא, Hashata hacha,

לַשָׁנָה הַבָּאָה lashana haba'a

בְּאַרְעָא דְיִשְׂרָאֵל. b'ar'a d'yisra'el.

הָשַׁתָּא עַבְדֵי, Hashata avdei,

לַשָׁנָה הַבָּאָה בְּנֵי חוֹרִין. lashana haba'a b'nei chorin.

♪
p. 100

This is the bread of affliction our ancestors ate
in the land of Egypt.

Let all who are hungry come and eat;
Let all who are in need come share
our Passover.

This year here,
next year in Israel;
today bound,
tomorrow free.

*   *

*This color denotes an optional reading

12

A fourth Matzah may be set aside for all who are separated from us against their will: the afflicted, the oppressed, the unfree, the 'prisoners of conscience'; and the following might then be recited:

צי דאַרף איך פֿײַערן דעם טאָג פֿון מײַן געבאָרן —

דאָס זאָלן זאָגן אַנדערע — זיי וייסן בעסער,

נאָר יענע שאָ פֿון טאָג, ווען כ׳בין באַפֿרײַט געוואָרן

פֿון הינטער שטעכנדיקן דראָט אין טפֿיסע־שלעסער,

די שאָ, וואָס אָנגעקומען איז זי אומדערווארט

מיט גליווערדיקן פֿראָסט אין אָנהייב כּוידעש מאַרט,

באַם הימל אויסגעשטערנטן אינמיטן טאָג,

און מיט דער בראָכע, וואָס איך האָב פֿון קינדווײַז

ניט געזאָגט, —

אָט יענער טאָג ווען ס׳קומט — איך רייד אַליין זיך אײַן:

בא יעדן מענטשן־פֿרײַנט די שאָ וועט יאָמטעוו זײַן,

ניט קלאַפֿנדיק אין טיר צו אים אין שטוב אַרײַן.

Should I celebrate the day of my birth?
Others know best—let them decide.
But that moment, the day they set me free
from the barbed wire of the prison-camp;
that hour not destined to arrive:
did come in early March, in Siberian frost
bright with stars at high noon.
That hour I recited the blessing
not spoken since childhood.
Now I persuade myself: such an hour, such a day
will be bestowed at last on every human friend.
That festal day
  will pass through every door
    without the need to knock.

*   *

The cups are refilled

13

The Four Questions

ארבע קשיות

To be asked by the youngest person(s) present

מַה־נִּשְׁתַּנָּה הַלַּיְלָה הַזֶּה

Ma nishtana halaila hazeh

מִכָּל־הַלֵּילוֹת?

mikol halailot?

שֶׁבְּכָל־הַלֵּילוֹת

Sheb'chol haleilot

אָנוּ אוֹכְלִין חָמֵץ וּמַצָּה,

anu och'lin chameitz u-matzah,

הַלַּיְלָה הַזֶּה כֻּלּוֹ מַצָּה.

halaila hazeh kulo matzah.

שֶׁבְּכָל־הַלֵּילוֹת

Sheb'chol haleilot

אָנוּ אוֹכְלִין שְׁאָר יְרָקוֹת,

anu och'lin sh'ar y'rakot,

הַלַּיְלָה הַזֶּה מָרוֹר.

halaila hazeh maror.

שֶׁבְּכָל־הַלֵּילוֹת

Sheb'chol haleilot

אֵין אָנוּ מַטְבִּילִין

ein anu matbilin

אֲפִלּוּ פַּעַם אֶחָת,

afilu pa-am echat,

הַלַּיְלָה הַזֶּה שְׁתֵּי פְעָמִים.

halaila hazeh sh'tei f'amim.

שֶׁבְּכָל־הַלֵּילוֹת

Sheb'chol haleilot

אָנוּ אוֹכְלִין בֵּין יוֹשְׁבִין

anu och'lin bein yosh'vin

וּבֵין מְסֻבִּין,

u-vein m'subin,

הַלַּיְלָה הַזֶּה כֻּלָּנוּ מְסֻבִּין.

halaila hazeh kulanu m'subin.

p. 101

Why is this night different from all other nights?
On other nights we eat bread leavened or unleavened:
on this night, unleavened only!
On other nights we eat all kinds of herbs:
on this night, bitter herbs!
On other nights we do not dip herbs at all:
on this night, twice!
On other nights we eat sitting upright or leaning:
on this night, we all lean!

*   *

All:

You are free to ask,
   you are free to question,
      free to learn the answers of tradition,
         free to add answers of your own!

*   *

14

The Four Children

ארבעה בנים

Leader:

The questions children ask,
the way they speak,
will tell you what they are like.
And parents should teach them
in accordance with their individual characters.

מִשְׁאֵלָתוֹ
וּמִדִּבּוּרוֹ
אַתָּה יוֹדֵעַ מַה־דַּעְתּוֹ.
וּלְפִי דַעְתּוֹ שֶׁל הַבֵּן
אָבִיו מְלַמְּדוֹ.

The Torah alludes	כְּנֶגֶד אַרְבָּעָה בָּנִים
to four types of child:	דִּבְּרָה תוֹרָה:
the wise,	אֶחָד חָכָם,
the wicked,	וְאֶחָד רָשָׁע,
the simple,	וְאֶחָד תָּם,
the one who does not know enough to ask.	וְאֶחָד שֶׁאֵינוֹ יוֹדֵעַ לִשְׁאוֹל.

What do wise children ask?	חָכָם מַה הוּא אוֹמֵר?

A Reader:

מָה הָעֵדֹת וְהַחֻקִּים וְהַמִּשְׁפָּטִים אֲשֶׁר צִוָּה יְיָ אֱלֹהֵינוּ
אוֹתָנוּ? וְאַף אַתָּה אֱמָר לוֹ כְּהִלְכוֹת הַפֶּסַח: אֵין מַפְטִירִין
אַחַר הַפֶּסַח אֲפִיקוֹמָן.

"What are the duties, laws, and rules that Adonai our God has taught us?" Such children should be taught the laws of Pesach from beginning to end, even this one: 'We conclude the Pesach meal with Afikoman.'

Leader:

What do the wicked ask?	רָשָׁע מַה הוּא אוֹמֵר?

A reader:

"What is this service to you?"	מָה הָעֲבוֹדָה הַזֹּאת לָכֶם?

לָכֶם וְלֹא לוֹ. וּלְפִי שֶׁהוֹצִיא אֶת־עַצְמוֹ מִן הַכְּלָל וְכָפַר
בָּעִקָּר, אַף אַתָּה הַקְהֵה אֶת־שִׁנָּיו וֶאֱמָר לוֹ: בַּעֲבוּר זֶה עָשָׂה
יְיָ לִי בְּצֵאתִי מִמִּצְרָיִם.

To *you* and not to *us!* Since they cut themselves off from the community and scorn our faith, make them eat their words, telling them: "I do this because of what God did for me when I came out of Egypt."

For *me* and not for *them.* Had	לִי וְלֹא לֹא:
they been there, they would	אִלּוּ הָיָה שָׁם
not have been redeemed.	לֹא הָיָה נִגְאָל.

16

Leader:

What does the simple one ask?

תָּם מַה הוּא אוֹמֵר?

A reader:

"What is this?

מַה־זֹּאת?

To that one say: "With a
mighty hand God led us
out of Egypt, out of the
house of bondage."

וְאָמַרְתָּ אֵלָיו:
בְּחֹזֶק יָד
הוֹצִיאָנוּ יְיָ מִמִּצְרַיִם
מִבֵּית עֲבָדִים.

All:

And with the one who does not
know enough to ask, you must
take the first step. As it
is said: "You shall tell
your child on that day . . ."

וְשֶׁאֵינוֹ יוֹדֵעַ לִשְׁאוֹל,
אַתְּ פְּתַח לוֹ,
שֶׁנֶּאֱמַר:
וְהִגַּדְתָּ לְבִנְךָ
בַּיּוֹם הַהוּא . . .

SUFFERING AND LOVE

Levi Yitzchak of Berditchev said: "The Haggadah speaks of four
children: the wise, the wicked, the simple, the one unable to ask. *I
am the one unable to ask.* But the parent of one unable to ask is
told: 'You must take the first step.' Ruler of the world, am I not
Your child? I do not ask to be told the secret of Your ways—I
could not bear it! But show me one thing: what You are telling me
through my life at this moment. I do not ask You to tell me *why* I
suffer, but only whether I suffer for Your sake!" (Chasidic)

THE WICKED CHILD

Our Rabbis have taught: When Israel is sunk in sorrow, and a Jew
stands apart from them, the two ministering angels that
accompany every one of us come and place their hands on that
person's head and say: "You have separated yourself from the
community; you will not see the consolation of the community."
(Talmud)

THE BASIC FREEDOM

Freedom is the freedom to say that two plus two make four. If
that is granted, all else follows. (George Orwell)

17

The Narration

Leader:

Our story begins with degradation;
our telling ends with glory.

מַתְחִיל (לְהַגִּיד) בִּגְנוּת;
וּמְסַיֵּם (לְסַפֵּר) בְּשֶׁבַח.

All:

עֲבָדִים הָיִינוּ לְפַרְעֹה בְּמִצְרָיִם. וַיּוֹצִיאֵנוּ יְיָ אֱלֹהֵינוּ מִשָּׁם
בְּיָד חֲזָקָה וּבִזְרוֹעַ נְטוּיָה. וְאִלּוּ לֹא הוֹצִיא הַקָּדוֹשׁ בָּרוּךְ
הוּא אֶת־אֲבוֹתֵינוּ מִמִּצְרַיִם, הֲרֵי אָנוּ וּבָנֵינוּ וּבְנֵי בָנֵינוּ
מְשֻׁעְבָּדִים הָיִינוּ לְפַרְעֹה בְּמִצְרָיִם.

We were slaves to Pharaoh in Egypt, and Adonai our
God led us out from there with a mighty hand, with an
outstretched arm. Had not the Holy One led our
ancestors out of Egypt, we and our children and our
children's children would still be enslaved.

Leader:

וַאֲפִלּוּ כֻּלָּנוּ חֲכָמִים, כֻּלָּנוּ נְבוֹנִים, כֻּלָּנוּ זְקֵנִים, כֻּלָּנוּ יוֹדְעִים
אֶת־הַתּוֹרָה, מִצְוָה עָלֵינוּ לְסַפֵּר בִּיצִיאַת מִצְרָיִם. וְכָל־
הַמַּרְבֶּה לְסַפֵּר בִּיצִיאַת מִצְרַיִם הֲרֵי זֶה מְשֻׁבָּח.

Therefore, even if all of us were wise, all discerning;
scholars, sages, and learned in Torah: we should still
have to tell the story of the Exodus. Praised is the one
who lingers over the telling!

A Reader:

מַעֲשֶׂה בְּרַבִּי אֱלִיעֶזֶר וְרַבִּי יְהוֹשֻׁעַ, וְרַבִּי אֶלְעָזָר בֶּן עֲזַרְיָה
וְרַבִּי עֲקִיבָא וְרַבִּי טַרְפוֹן, שֶׁהָיוּ מְסֻבִּין בִּבְנֵי בְרַק, וְהָיוּ
מְסַפְּרִים בִּיצִיאַת מִצְרַיִם כָּל־אוֹתוֹ הַלַּיְלָה, עַד שֶׁבָּאוּ
תַלְמִידֵיהֶם וְאָמְרוּ לָהֶם: רַבּוֹתֵינוּ, הִגִּיעַ זְמַן קְרִיאַת שְׁמַע
שֶׁל שַׁחֲרִית!

They say that Rabbi Eliezer, Rabbi Joshua, Rabbi Elazar
ben Azariah, Rabbi Akiba, and Rabbi Tarfon were
sitting at the Seder table in B'nei B'rak; all that night

18

they talked about the Exodus, until their students came and said to them: "Rabbis, it is time to recite the morning Shema!"

אָמַר רַבִּי אֶלְעָזָר בֶּן־עֲזַרְיָה: הֲרֵי אֲנִי כְּבֶן שִׁבְעִים שָׁנָה. וְלֹא זָכִיתִי שֶׁתֵּאָמֵר יְצִיאַת מִצְרַיִם בַּלֵּילוֹת, עַד שֶׁדְּרָשָׁה בֶּן זוֹמָא. שֶׁנֶּאֱמַר: לְמַעַן תִּזְכֹּר אֶת־יוֹם צֵאתְךָ מֵאֶרֶץ מִצְרַיִם כֹּל יְמֵי חַיֶּיךָ. יְמֵי חַיֶּיךָ: הַיָּמִים. כֹּל יְמֵי חַיֶּיךָ: הַלֵּילוֹת. וַחֲכָמִים אוֹמְרִים: יְמֵי חַיֶּיךָ: הָעוֹלָם הַזֶּה. כֹּל יְמֵי חַיֶּיךָ: לְהָבִיא לִימוֹת הַמָּשִׁיחַ.

Rabbi Elazar ben Azariah said: I seem like a man of seventy, yet I never understood why we must tell of the Exodus at night until Ben Zoma came along with this teaching: "Remember the day you went out of Egypt all the days of your life" (Deuteronomy 16.3). It is easy to remember your liberation when the sun is shining. But you must remember it *all the days of your life*—even when the sun has set, even when your day is dark.

The Sages saw an additional lesson in this verse: "The days of your life" are your days in this world—the world as it is; "*all* the days of your life" includes the messianic day. Let your remembrance of liberation help change the world as it is into the world as it ought to be.

Our story begins with degradation; our telling ends with glory.

מַתְחִיל (לְהַגִּיד) בִּגְנוּת; וּמְסַיֵּים (לְסַפֵּר) בְּשֶׁבַח.

מִתְּחִלָּה עוֹבְדֵי עֲבוֹדָה זָרָה הָיוּ אֲבוֹתֵינוּ, וְעַכְשָׁו קֵרְבָנוּ הַמָּקוֹם לַעֲבוֹדָתוֹ, שֶׁנֶּאֱמַר: וַיֹּאמֶר יְהוֹשֻׁעַ אֶל־כָּל־הָעָם, כֹּה־אָמַר יְיָ אֱלֹהֵי יִשְׂרָאֵל, בְּעֵבֶר הַנָּהָר יָשְׁבוּ אֲבוֹתֵיכֶם מֵעוֹלָם, תֶּרַח אֲבִי אַבְרָהָם וַאֲבִי נָחוֹר, וַיַּעַבְדוּ אֱלֹהִים

אֲחֵרִים. וָאֶקַּח אֶת־אֲבִיכֶם אֶת־אַבְרָהָם מֵעֵבֶר הַנָּהָר,
וָאוֹלֵךְ אוֹתוֹ בְּכָל־אֶרֶץ כְּנָעַן, וָאַרְבֶּה אֶת־זַרְעוֹ, וָאֶתֶּן לוֹ
אֶת־יִצְחָק, וָאֶתֵּן לְיִצְחָק אֶת־יַעֲקֹב וְאֶת־עֵשָׂו, וָאֶתֵּן לְעֵשָׂו
אֶת־הַר שֵׂעִיר לָרֶשֶׁת אוֹתוֹ, וְיַעֲקֹב וּבָנָיו יָרְדוּ מִצְרָיִם.

In the beginning our ancestors served idols; now we
are called to serve the Divine. As it is said: "Thus says
Adonai, the God of Israel, 'Long ago your ancestors
lived beyond the River Eurphrates and served other
gods. Then I took Abraham and Sarah from beyond the
River, and led them all over the land of Canaan. I
multiplied their descendants . . . and let Esau take
possession of Mount Seir. But Jacob and his children
went down to Egypt.'"

Our story begins with degradation; our telling ends with glory.	מַתְחִיל (לְהַגִּיד) בִּגְנוּת; וּמְסַיֵּם (לְסַפֵּר) בְּשֶׁבַח.

All:

Our ancestors were wandering Arameans.	אֲרַמִּי אֹבֵד אָבִי.
They went down to Egypt.	וַיֵּרֶד מִצְרַיְמָה.
They lived there as strangers, few in number.	וַיָּגָר שָׁם בִּמְתֵי מְעָט.
There they became a great nation, mighty and numerous.	וַיְהִי שָׁם לְגוֹי גָּדוֹל, עָצוּם וָרָב.
But the Egyptians were cruel to us.	וַיָּרֵעוּ אֹתָנוּ הַמִּצְרִים.
They afflicted us.	וַיְעַנּוּנוּ.
They imposed hard labor upon us.	וַיִּתְּנוּ עָלֵינוּ עֲבֹדָה קָשָׁה.
Then we cried out to Adonai, the God of our ancestors.	וַנִּצְעַק אֶל יְיָ אֱלֹהֵי אֲבֹתֵינוּ.
And the Eternal heard our cry, saw our plight, our woe, our oppression.	וַיִּשְׁמַע יְיָ אֶת־קֹלֵנוּ, וַיַּרְא אֶת־עָנְיֵנוּ וְאֶת־עֲמָלֵנוּ וְאֶת־לַחֲצֵנוּ.
Then God led us out of Egypt with a mighty hand, with an outstretched arm, with awesome power, with signs and wonders.	וַיּוֹצִיאֵנוּ יְיָ מִמִּצְרַיִם בְּיָד חֲזָקָה וּבִזְרֹעַ נְטוּיָה, וּבְמֹרָא גָדוֹל וּבְאֹתוֹת וּבְמֹפְתִים.

20

The following section may be omitted,
if many very young children are present.
This section ends on page 27.

Midrash מדרש

The Exodus in Detail יציאת מצרים בפרט

Leader:

OUR ANCESTORS WERE WANDERING ARAMEANS   אֲרַמִּי אֹבֵד אָבִי

All:

We began as wanderers, without a home. Again and yet again, we have been wanderers, fugitives, refugees.

Leader:

THEY WENT DOWN TO EGYPT   וַיֵּרֶד מִצְרַיְמָה

A Reader:

Though upon our arrival there we were made welcome in the land of Egypt, in the end our 'going down' was a descent into degradation. Not only were we enslaved, but we *accepted* our lot: when first we heard the divine promise of liberation, we would not listen, "because of our broken spirit."

THE HABIT OF BONDAGE

My very chains and I grew friends,
So much a long communion tends
To make us what we are:—even I
Regain'd my freedom with a sigh.   (Lord Byron)

THE REAL SLAVERY

The real slavery of Israel in Egypt was that they had learned to endure it. (Chasidic)

"WHO HAS NOT MADE ME A SLAVE"

Jewish resistance in the concentration camps took many forms. For some, it consisted of a refusal to allow themselves to feel degraded, even in the worst of circumstances. There were Jews who continued to live by Halachah—Jewish Law—even there.

21

One such Jew addressed a question to Rabbi Ephraim Oshry: "Should a Jew, having to do forced labor for the Nazis, continue to recite the benediction in the morning service, "We praise You, Adonai our God, Ruler of time and space, who has not made me a slave"? Rabbi Oshry answered: "Heaven forbid that they should give up reciting the *B'rachah* that was established by the great sages of yesteryear. On the contrary, now of all times we are obliged to say this *B'rachah*, so that our adversaries and tormentors realize that, although we are in their power to do with us as their wicked machinations devise, we nonetheless perceive ourselves not as slaves, but as free people, prisoners for the time being, whose liberation will soon come and whose deliverance will quickly be accomplished." (Albert Axelrad)

Leader:

THEY LIVED THERE AS STRANGERS
FEW IN NUMBER

וַיָּגָר שָׁם
בִּמְתֵי מְעָט

A Reader:

בְּשִׁבְעִים נֶפֶשׁ יָרְדוּ אֲבֹתֶיךָ מִצְרָיְמָה, וְעַתָּה שָׂמְךָ יְיָ אֱלֹהֶיךָ כְּכוֹכְבֵי הַשָּׁמַיִם לָרֹב.

"Our ancestors who entered Egypt numbered only seventy, and now Adonai our God has made us as numerous as the stars of heaven."

Leader:

THEY BECAME A GREAT NATION

וַיְהִי שָׁם לְגוֹי גָּדוֹל

The use of the word 'nation' shows that they remained true to themselves.

"וַיְהִי שָׁם לְגוֹי" מְלַמֵּד שֶׁהָיוּ יִשְׂרָאֵל מְצֻיָּנִים שָׁם.

How did Israel show its self-respect? We have learned:

הִצְטַיְנוּתוֹ שֶׁל עַם יִשְׂרָאֵל מַהִי?

This people is truly itself when it displays three virtues:

שְׁלֹשָׁה סִימָנִים יֵשׁ בְּאוּמָה זוֹ:

compassion, modesty, and kindness.

הָרַחֲמָנִים וְהַבַּיְשָׁנִים וְגוֹמְלֵי חֲסָדִים.

22

Leader:

MIGHTY AND NUMEROUS

עָצוּם וָרָב

All:

"The people of Israel were fruitful,
their numbers increased rapidly
until the land was full of them."

וּבְנֵי יִשְׂרָאֵל פָּרוּ וַיִּשְׁרְצוּ,
וַיִּרְבּוּ וַיַּעַצְמוּ בִּמְאֹד מְאֹד,
וַתִּמָּלֵא הָאָרֶץ אֹתָם.

Leader:

BUT THE EGYPTIANS WERE CRUEL TO US

וַיָּרֵעוּ אֹתָנוּ הַמִּצְרִים

A Reader:

וַיָּקָם מֶלֶךְ חָדָשׁ עַל מִצְרָיִם, אֲשֶׁר לֹא יָדַע אֶת־יוֹסֵף. וַיֹּאמֶר
אֶל־עַמּוֹ: הִנֵּה עַם בְּנֵי יִשְׂרָאֵל רַב וְעָצוּם מִמֶּנּוּ. הָבָה
נִתְחַכְּמָה לוֹ, פֶּן יִרְבֶּה וְהָיָה כִּי תִקְרֶאנָה מִלְחָמָה וְנוֹסַף גַּם
הוּא עַל שֹׂנְאֵינוּ, וְנִלְחַם־בָּנוּ, וְעָלָה מִן הָאָרֶץ.

As it is said: "Now a new king rose over Egypt, who 'did
not know' Joseph. He said to his people, 'Behold, this
people Israel is far too numerous for comfort. Let us
now deal shrewdly with them, lest they continue to
increase and, in the event of war, join our enemies and
fight against us, and then escape from the land.'"

SHIFRAH AND PUAH

Two women provide us with the first recorded example of
spiritual resistance to tyranny. Shifrah and Puah were the
midwives ordered by Pharaoh to kill all male children born to
Israelite women. "But the midwives feared God and did not do as
the King of Egypt had told them, but kept the infants alive"
(Exodus 1.17).

Pharaoh sought to conceal his responsibility for his genocidal plan
by acting through what might seem innocent intermediaries—the
midwives—as though by this means the deaths would appear to be
natural. But Shifrah and Puah did not allow him to escape the
consequences of his acts. Their moral courage is a model of
responsible ethical behavior. (Exodus Rabbah 1.14)

"(They) did not do as the King of Egypt had told them, but kept
the infants alive." Strictly speaking the second half of this

sentence is superfluous: once we are told that the midwives did not do the bidding of Pharaoh, we *know* they kept the infants alive. Why then does the Torah add these words? To add to the praise of these women—for keeping them alive means more than not putting them to death. After the birth of these infants, Shifrah and Puah *sustained* them, bringing food and drink to those who had none by reason of their poverty. (Exodus Rabbah 1.15, expanded)

TO STRUGGLE FOR FREEDOM

Covey at length let me go, puffing and blowing at a great rate, saying that if I had not resisted, he would not have whipped me half so much. The truth was, that he had not whipped me at all. I considered him as getting entirely the worst end of the bargain; for he had drawn no blood from me, but I had from him. The whole six months afterwards, that I spent with Mr. Covey, he never laid the weight of his finger upon me.

This battle with Mr. Covey was the turning-point of my career as a slave. It rekindled the few expiring embers of freedom, and revived within me a sense of my own manhood.

It was a glorious resurrection, from the tomb of slavery, to the heaven of freedom. (Frederick Douglass)

Leader:

THEY AFFLICTED US   וַיְעַנּוּנוּ

A Reader:

וַיָּשִׂימוּ עָלָיו שָׂרֵי מִסִּים, לְמַעַן עַנֹּתוֹ בְּסִבְלֹתָם, וַיִּבֶן עָרֵי
מִסְכְּנוֹת לְפַרְעֹה, אֶת־פִּתֹם וְאֶת־רַעַמְסֵס.

As it is said: "They set taskmasters over them, to afflict them with forced labor; thus they built for Pharaoh store-cities, such as Pithom and Raamses."

Leader:

THEY IMPOSED HARD LABOR UPON US   וַיִּתְּנוּ עָלֵינוּ עֲבֹדָה קָשָׁה

25

וַיַּעֲבִידוּ מִצְרַיִם אֶת־בְּנֵי יִשְׂרָאֵל בְּפָרֶךְ. שָׁנִינוּ: מְלַמֵּד שֶׁהָיוּ
בְּיָדָם מְגִלוֹת, שֶׁהָיוּ מִשְׁתַּעַשְׁעִין בָּהֶן מִשַּׁבָּת לְשַׁבָּת, לֵאמֹר
שֶׁהַקָּדוֹשׁ בָּרוּךְ הוּא גּוֹאֲלָם, לְפִי שֶׁהָיוּ נוֹחִין בְּשַׁבָּת. אָמַר
לָהֶם פַּרְעֹה: תִּכְבַּד הָעֲבוֹדָה עַל הָאֲנָשִׁים וְיַעֲשׂוּ־בָהּ וְאַל
יִשְׁעוּ בְּדִבְרֵי־שָׁקֶר — אַל יְהוּ מִשְׁתַּעַשְׁעִין וְאַל יִהְיוּ נְפֶשִׁים
בְּיוֹם הַשַּׁבָּת.

As it is said: "The Egyptians ruthlessly imposed hard
labor upon the people of Israel." And we have learned:

During the bondage, Israel kept its traditions alive. Each Shabbat their spirits would revive: the Holy One *would* redeem them! So Pharaoh decreed: "Make their work harder; destroy their false hopes"—Let them not have Sabbaths on which to refresh themselves.

Leader:

THEN WE CRIED OUT TO ADONAI,
    THE GOD OF OUR ANCESTORS

וַנִּצְעַק אֶל יְיָ
אֱלֹהֵי אֲבֹתֵינוּ

A Reader:

וַיְהִי בַיָּמִים הָרַבִּים הָהֵם, וַיָּמָת מֶלֶךְ מִצְרַיִם, וַיֵּאָנְחוּ בְנֵי יִשְׂרָאֵל מִן הָעֲבֹדָה וַיִּזְעָקוּ; וַתַּעַל שַׁוְעָתָם אֶל הָאֱלֹהִים מִן הָעֲבֹדָה.

As it is said: "During those long, painful days, the king of Egypt died. But the people of Israel still groaned under their bondage, and cried out; and the screams wrung from them by their bondage ascended to God."

Leader:

AND THE ETERNAL HEARD OUR CRY

וַיִּשְׁמַע יְיָ אֶת־קוֹלֵנוּ

All:

As it is said: "God heard
their groans, and God
remembered the covenant . . ."

וַיִּשְׁמַע אֱלֹהִים אֶת־
נַאֲקָתָם, וַיִּזְכֹּר אֱלֹהִים
אֶת־בְּרִיתוֹ . . .

A Reader:

And that covenant was made with Abraham and with Sarah, with Isaac and Rebekah, with Jacob, Leah and Rachel, with every member of the House of Israel. It belongs to all ages, all women, all men; it belongs to the children and to the grandparents. It belongs to all of us, even the generations waiting to be born.

Leader:

AND (THE ETERNAL) SAW   וַיַּרְא . . .

A Reader:

We have learned: God saw that the slaves showed compassion for one another; upon completing their own work-quotas, they would go help the others.

מֶה רָאָה יְיָ? שֶׁהָיוּ מְרַחֲמִים זֶה עַל זֶה. כְּשֶׁהָיָה אֶחָד מֵהֶם מַשְׁלִים סְכוּם הַלְּבֵנִים קֹדֶם חֲבֵרוֹ, הָיָה בָא וּמְסַיֵּעַ לוֹ.

Leader:

AND THE ETERNAL SAW . . .
What did the Holy One see?

וַיַּרְא . . .
מֶה רָאָה הַקָּדוֹשׁ בָּרוּךְ הוּא?

A Reader:

It is said: "And God saw the people of Israel, and God knew . . ."

וַיַּרְא אֱלֹהִים אֶת־
בְּנֵי יִשְׂרָאֵל וַיֵּדַע אֱלֹהִים . . .

All:

God saw: the enforced separation of husbands and wives.

וַיַּרְא יְיָ: זוֹ פְּרִישׁוּת דֶּרֶךְ אֶרֶץ.

A Reader:

It is said: "Every son that is born you shall throw into the Nile."

כָּל־הַבֵּן הַיִּלּוֹד הַיְאֹרָה תַּשְׁלִיכֻהוּ . . .

All:

God saw: the murder of our children.

וַיַּרְא יְיָ: אֵלֶּה הַבָּנִים.

A Reader:

And it is said: "Moreover, I have seen how the Egyptians oppress them."

וְגַם רָאִיתִי אֶת־הַלַּחַץ אֲשֶׁר מִצְרַיִם לֹחֲצִים אֹתָם.

All:

God saw: the determination to crush our spirit.

וַיַּרְא יְיָ: שֶׁגָּזַר פַּרְעֹה לְהַכְנִיעַ וּלְהַשְׁפִּיל רוּחֵנוּ.

Leader:

AND THE ETERNAL SAW OUR PLIGHT

וַיַּרְא אֶת־עָנְיֵנוּ

A Reader:

God said: "How well I see the plight of My people in Egypt; I hear their outcry against their taskmasters; Yes, I know how they suffer."

וַיֹּאמֶר יְיָ: רָאֹה רָאִיתִי אֶת־עֳנִי עַמִּי אֲשֶׁר בְּמִצְרָיִם, וְאֶת־צַעֲקָתָם שָׁמַעְתִּי מִפְּנֵי נֹגְשָׂיו, כִּי יָדַעְתִּי אֶת־מַכְאֹבָיו.

Leader:

OUR PLIGHT, OUR WOE,
    OUR OPPRESSION

אֶת־עָנְיֵנוּ וְאֶת־עֲמָלֵנוּ וְאֶת־לַחֲצֵנוּ

A Reader:

Our plight is God's as well, for we are taught: "God is diminished when we are oppressed." And it is written: "In all their afflictions, God is afflicted."

כְּנֶגֶד הַקָּדוֹשׁ בָּרוּךְ הוּא דִּבְּרָה הַתּוֹרָה, כַּכָּתוּב: וַתִּקְצַר נַפְשׁוֹ בַּעֲמַל יִשְׂרָאֵל. וְעוֹד: בְּכָל־צָרָתָם לוֹ צָר.

A Reader:

And we have learned:
Whenever we go into exile,
the Divine Presence goes with us.
When we were exiled to Egypt,
the Divine Presence went with us;
in Babylon the Presence was with us;
and until the final redemption,
God will remain in exile with us.

וְשָׁנִינוּ:
בְּכָל־מָקוֹם שֶׁגָּלוּ,
שְׁכִינָה עִמָּהֶן.
גָּלוּ לְמִצְרָיִם,
שְׁכִינָה עִמָּהֶן;
גָּלוּ לְבָבֶל, שְׁכִינָה עִמָּהֶן;
וְאַף כְּשֶׁהֵן עֲתִידִין לִיגָּאֵל,
שְׁכִינָה עִמָּהֶן.

THE 'WAGE-SLAVE'—OUR PLIGHT

Even if you are a slave, forced to labour at some abominable and murderous trade for bread—as iron-forging, for instance, or gunpowder-making—you can resolve to deliver yourself, and your children after you, from the chains of that hell, and from the domination of its slavemasters, or to die.... What Egyptian bondage do you suppose ... was ever so cruel as a modern

English forge, with its steel hammers? What Egyptian worship of garlic or crocodile ever so damnable as modern English worship of money? (John Ruskin)

THE 'BENEVOLENT' DESPOT—OUR WOE

I sit on a man's back, choking him and making him carry me, and yet assure myself and others that I am very sorry for him and wish to lighten his load by all possible means—except by getting off his back. (Leo Tolstoi)

POWER OVER WOMEN—OUR OPPRESSION

The less fit a man is for the possession of power—the less likely to be allowed to exercise it over any person with that person's voluntary consent—the more does he hug himself in the consciousness of the power the law gives him, exact its legal rights to the utmost point which custom (the custom of men like himself) will tolerate, and take pleasure in using the power, merely to enliven the agreeable sense of possessing it. (John Stuart Mill)

Leader:

THEN GOD LED US OUT OF EGYPT	וַיּוֹצִיאֵנוּ יְיָ מִמִּצְרַיִם
WITH A MIGHTY HAND,	בְּיָד חֲזָקָה,
WITH AN OUTSTRETCHED ARM	וּבִזְרֹעַ נְטוּיָה

All:

Not by an angel.	לֹא עַל יְדֵי מַלְאָךְ.
Not by a seraph.	וְלֹא עַל יְדֵי שָׂרָף.
Not by a messenger.	וְלֹא עַל יְדֵי שָׁלִיחַ.
You Yourself,	אֶלָּא
the Holy One,	הַקָּדוֹשׁ בָּרוּךְ הוּא
in all Your glory!	בִּכְבוֹדוֹ וּבְעַצְמוֹ!

Leader:

WITH AWESOME POWER, WITH SIGNS	וּבְמֹרָא גָּדוֹל, וּבְאֹתוֹת
AND WONDERS	וּבְמוֹפְתִים

A Reader:

זוֹ גִּלּוּי שְׁכִינָה: כְּמוֹ שֶׁנֶּאֱמַר, אוֹ הֲנִסָּה אֱלֹהִים, לָבוֹא
לָקַחַת לוֹ גוֹי מִקֶּרֶב גּוֹי, בְּמַסֹּת, בְּאֹתֹת וּבְמוֹפְתִים

30

וּבְמִלְחָמָה, וּבְיָד חֲזָקָה וּבִזְרוֹעַ נְטוּיָה, וּבְמוֹרָאִים גְּדֹלִים,
כְּכֹל אֲשֶׁר עָשָׂה לָכֶם יְיָ אֱלֹהֵיכֶם, בְּמִצְרַיִם לְעֵינֶיךָ?

The Divine Presence reveals itself as liberation. As it is said: "Has any 'god' ever attempted to go and take a nation from the very midst of another nation with awesome power, with signs and wonders, as Adonai your God did for you in Egypt before your very eyes?"

Leader:

No liberation is easy. As tyranny brings death and terror to its victims, so the struggle to overthrow it claims its casualties. There is no redemption without pain.

Israel suffered greatly before it was redeemed from Egyptian bondage. And we remember that our oppressors suffered many plagues before they were willing to let our people go.

Our rejoicing at the liberation of our ancestors should be tempered by the memory of this suffering of the oppressor and the oppressed, and by the knowledge that tyranny and cruelty still abide: tyrants fall but others rise to take their place. Many evils remain to plague us. Each one diminishes our cup of joy.

All:

A pathy in the face of evil
B rutal torture of the helpless
C ruel mockery of the old and the weak
D espair of human goodness
E nvy of the joy of others
F alsehood and deception corroding our faith
G reedy theft of earth's resources
H atred of learning and culture
I nstigation of war and aggression
J ustice delayed, justice denied, justice mocked . . .

Leader:

We look back now upon the ancient plagues, the plagues of legend, the signs and wonders that haunt us still:

A drop of wine is removed from the cup
at the mention of each plague

31

עשר מכות

All:

דָּם Dam

צְפַרְדֵּעַ Ts'fardei-a

כִּנִּים Kinim

עָרוֹב Arov

דֶּבֶר Dever

שְׁחִין Sh'chin

בָּרָד Barad

אַרְבֶּה Arbeh

חֹשֶׁךְ Choshech

מַכַּת בְּכוֹרוֹת Makat B'chorot

The Ten Plagues

All:

BLOOD

FROGS

LICE

FLIES

CATTLE DISEASE

BOILS

HAIL

LOCUSTS

DARKNESS

DEATH OF THE FIRSTBORN

The experiences of camp life show that man does have a choice of action. There were enough examples, often of a heroic nature, which proved that apathy could be overcome, irritability suppressed. Man can preserve a vestige of spiritual freedom, of independence of mind, even in such terrible conditions of psychic stress. We who lived in concentration camps can remember the men who walked through the huts comforting others, giving away their last piece of bread. They may have been few in number, but they offer sufficient proof that everything can be taken from a man but one thing: the last of the human freedoms— to choose one's attitude in any given set of circumstances, to choose one's own way. (Victor Frankl)

Leader:

When the cup of suffering had run over, Egypt's grip was loosened. On that day, Israel went forth to freedom. They made their way to the Sea of Reeds. Cloud by day, fire by night: God's Presence went before them. Pharaoh's heart changed yet again, and he dispatched his troops to recapture the fleeing slaves—for the oppressors' fury grows as their grip begins to weaken, and in their rage they pursue their victims even to their own destruction. Israel stood uncertain: before them the Sea, behind them Egypt's host.

A Reader:

כְּשֶׁעָמְדוּ יִשְׂרָאֵל עַל הַיָּם, הָיָה זֶה אוֹמֵר: אֵין אֲנִי יוֹרֵד תְּחִלָּה לַיָּם, וְזֶה אוֹמֵר: אֵין אֲנִי יוֹרֵד תְּחִלָּה לַיָּם. מִתּוֹךְ שֶׁהָיוּ עוֹמְדִין וְנוֹטְלִין עֵצָה אֵלּוּ וָאֵלּוּ, קָפַץ נַחְשׁוֹן בֶּן עַמִּינָדָב וְיָרַד לַיָּם תְּחִלָּה.

AT THAT TIME, when Israel stood at the edge of the sea, each one said, 'I will not be the first to enter.' While they stood there, Nachshon ben Amminadav leaped into the sea. Only then did the others follow.

A Reader:

בְּשָׁעָה שֶׁיָּרְדוּ יִשְׂרָאֵל לַיָּם, 'בָּאוּ מַיִם עַד נָפֶשׁ'. מִכָּאן אַתָּה לָמֵד, שֶׁלֹּא נִקְרַע לָהֶם הַיָּם עַד שֶׁבָּאוּ לְתוֹכוֹ עַד חָטְמָן, וְאַחַר־כָּךְ נַעֲשָׂה לָהֶם יַבָּשָׁה.

34

AT THAT TIME, they plunged into the waters, going further and further, until it seemed the waters must cover their heads. Only when they had gone as far as they could through their own efforts, did the waters part for them!

Leader:

The people overcame their fear, as all must in every generation who would be free. For the human fate has been exile and oppression, again and again; and the human task: to find hope, to overcome. As it is said:

All:

אַל תִּירָא, כִּי גְאַלְתִּיךָ; קָרָאתִי בְשִׁמְךָ, לִי אֶתָּה. כִּי תַעֲבוֹר בַּמַּיִם, אִתְּךָ אֲנִי; וּבַנְּהָרוֹת, לֹא יִשְׁטְפוּךָ.

"Have no fear, for I am redeeming you; I have called you by name, you are Mine. When you pass through the waters, I am with you; when you pass through the torrents, they shall not overwhelm you."

Leader:

וַיַּרְא יִשְׂרָאֵל אֶת־הַיָּד הַגְּדֹלָה אֲשֶׁר עָשָׂה יְיָ בְּמִצְרַיִם, וַיִּירְאוּ הָעָם אֶת־יְיָ . . .

בְּאוֹתָהּ שָׁעָה בִּקְשׁוּ מַלְאֲכֵי הַשָּׁרֵת לוֹמַר שִׁירָה לִפְנֵי הַקָּדוֹשׁ בָּרוּךְ הוּא. אָמַר לָהֶם הַקָּדוֹשׁ בָּרוּךְ הוּא: מַעֲשֵׂי יָדַי טוֹבְעִין בַּיָּם וְאַתֶּם אוֹמְרִים שִׁירָה לְפָנַי!

It is said: "When Israel saw the great deed the Eternal had done against the Egyptians, the people stood in awe of God . . ."

AT THAT TIME, the ministering angels began to sing a song of praise before the Holy One; but God rebuked them, saying, 'My children are drowning, and you sing praises!"

*   *

O God, teach us to rejoice in freedom,
but not in its cost for us and our enemies.
Let there come a day when violence is no more,
and we shall be free to rejoice without sadness,
to sing without tears.

Leader:

That day is not yet. Since the Exodus we have known many oppressions and deliverances. Often we have suffered, often triumphed—and always, as a people, survived. For the Redeemer of Israel has been our never-failing strength. As it is said:

A Reader:

"Fear not, for I am with you;
אַל תִּירָא, כִּי עִמְּךָ אָנִי;

do not despair, for I am your God.
אַל תִּשְׁתָּע, כִּי אֲנִי אֱלֹהֶיךָ.

I will strengthen you;
אִמַּצְתִּיךָ,

I will help you;
אַף עֲזַרְתִּיךָ;

I will uphold you
אַף תְּמַכְתִּיךָ

with the power of My hand!"
בִּימִין צִדְקִי!

The cups are raised

All:

Blessed is the One who keeps faith
בָּרוּךְ שׁוֹמֵר הַבְטָחָתוֹ לְיִשְׂרָאֵל,

with Israel; blessed is our God.
בָּרוּךְ הוּא.

This promise sustained our ancestors;
וְהִיא שֶׁעָמְדָה לַאֲבוֹתֵינוּ

this promise sustains us.
וְלֶנוּ.

For not only one enemy has sought
שֶׁלֹּא אֶחָד בִּלְבַד

to destroy us:
עָמַד עָלֵינוּ לְכַלּוֹתֵינוּ:

in every generation there are those
אֶלָּא שֶׁבְּכָל־דּוֹר וָדוֹר

who seek to destroy us,
עוֹמְדִים עָלֵינוּ לְכַלּוֹתֵינוּ,

but the Holy One saves us
וְהַקָּדוֹשׁ בָּרוּךְ הוּא

from their hands.
מַצִּילֵנוּ מִיָּדָם.

The cups are set down

Leader:

בְּכָל־דּוֹר וָדוֹר חַיָּב אָדָם לִרְאוֹת אֶת־עַצְמוֹ כְּאִלּוּ הוּא יָצָא
מִמִּצְרַיִם, שֶׁנֶּאֱמַר: וְהִגַּדְתָּ לְבִנְךָ בַּיּוֹם הַהוּא לֵאמֹר, בַּעֲבוּר
זֶה עָשָׂה יְיָ לִי בְּצֵאתִי מִמִּצְרָיִם.

In each generation, every one of us must feel that he,
that she, has personally gone out of Egypt. As it is said:
"You shall tell your child on that day, 'I do this because
of what God did for *me* when I came out of Egypt.'"

All:

לֹא אֶת־אֲבוֹתֵינוּ בִּלְבָד גָּאַל הַקָּדוֹשׁ בָּרוּךְ הוּא, אֶלָּא אַף
אוֹתָנוּ גָּאַל עִמָּהֶם, שֶׁנֶּאֱמַר: וְאוֹתָנוּ הוֹצִיא מִשָּׁם, לְמַעַן
הָבִיא אֹתָנוּ לָתֵת לָנוּ אֶת־הָאָרֶץ אֲשֶׁר נִשְׁבַּע לַאֲבֹתֵינוּ.

For the Holy One redeemed not only our ancestors,
but us along with them. As it is said: "You led *us* out of
there, that you might bring us to the land You promised to our ancestors."

*   *

THE SLAVEHOLDER IS NOT FREE

If you put a chain around the neck of a slave, the other end fastens
itself around your own. (Ralph Waldo Emerson)

THE PRICE OF INJUSTICE

Whatever the human law may be, neither an individual nor a
nation can ever *deliberately* commit the least act of injustice without
having to pay the penalty for it. (Henry David Thoreau)

DO NOT BECOME THE ENEMY

Whoever battles with monsters had better see to it that it does not
turn him into a monster. And if you gaze long into an abyss, the
abyss will gaze back into you. (Friedrich Nietzsche)

37

Dayyenu דַּיֵּנוּ

How many gifts
has God bestowed on us!

כַּמָּה מַעֲלוֹת טוֹבוֹת
לַמָּקוֹם עָלֵינוּ!

♪

p. 101

אִלּוּ הוֹצִיאָנוּ מִמִּצְרַיִם
וְלֹא סִפֵּק צָרְכֵּנוּ בַּמִּדְבָּר —
דַּיֵּנוּ!

Ilu hotsi-anu mimitsrayim
v'lo sipeik tsorkeinu bamidbar—
dayyenu!

אִלּוּ סִפֵּק צָרְכֵּנוּ בַּמִּדְבָּר
וְלֹא נָתַן לָנוּ אֶת־הַשַּׁבָּת —
דַּיֵּנוּ!

Ilu sipeik tsorkeinu bamidbar
v'lo natan lanu et hashabbat—
dayyenu!

אִלּוּ נָתַן לָנוּ אֶת־הַשַּׁבָּת
וְלֹא נָתַן לָנוּ אֶת־הַתּוֹרָה —
דַּיֵּנוּ!

Ilu natan lanu et hashabbat
v'lo natan lanu et hatorah—
dayyenu!

אִלּוּ נָתַן לָנוּ אֶת־הַתּוֹרָה
וְלֹא הִכְנִיסָנוּ לְאֶרֶץ יִשְׂרָאֵל —
דַּיֵּנוּ!

Ilu natan lanu et hatorah
v'lo hichnisanu l'erets Yisrael—
dayyenu!

אִלּוּ הִכְנִיסָנוּ לְאֶרֶץ יִשְׂרָאֵל
וְלֹא שָׁלַח לָנוּ אֶת־הַנְּבִיאִים —
דַּיֵּנוּ!

Ilu hichnisanu l'erets Yisrael
v'lo shalach lanu et ha-n'vi-im—
dayyenu!

אִלּוּ שָׁלַח לָנוּ אֶת־הַנְּבִיאִים
וְלֹא נְתָנָנוּ לְאוֹר גּוֹיִים —
דַּיֵּנוּ!

Ilu shalach lanu et ha-n'vi-im
v'lo n'tananu l'or go-yim—
dayyenu!

אִלּוּ נְתָנָנוּ לְאוֹר גּוֹיִים
וְלֹא הֶחֱיָנוּ בְּכָל־אַרְצוֹת
תְּפוּצָתֵנוּ —
דַּיֵּנוּ!

Ilu n'tananu l'or go-yim
v'lo hecheyanu b'chol artsot
t'futsateinu—
dayyenu!

אִלּוּ הֶחֱיָנוּ בְּכָל־אַרְצוֹת
תְּפוּצָתֵנוּ —
וְלֹא הֱשִׁיבָנוּ
לְאֶרֶץ אֲבוֹתֵינוּ —
דַּיֵּנוּ!

Ilu hecheyanu b'chol artsot
t'futsateinu—
v'lo heshivanu
l'erets avoteinu—
dayyenu!

39

אִלוּ הֱשִׁיבָנוּ לְאֶרֶץ אֲבוֹתֵינוּ Ilu heshivanu l'erets avoteinu
וְלֹא צִוָּנוּ v'lo tsivanu
לְתַקֵּן עוֹלָמוֹ— l'takein olamo—
דַּיֵּנוּ! dayyeinu!

Had God brought us out of Egypt and not supported us in the wilderness—

It would have been enough!

Had God supported us in the wilderness and not given us the Sabbath—

It would have been enough!

Had God given us the Sabbath and not given us the Torah—

It would have been enough!

Had God given us the Torah and not brought us to the land of Israel—

It would have been enough!

Had God brought us to the land of Israel and not sent us the prophets—

It would have been enough!

Had God sent us the prophets and not called us to be a light to the nations—

It would have been enough!

Had God called us to be a light to the nations and not sustained us wherever we have dwelt—

It would have been enough!

Had God sustained us wherever we have dwelt and not returned us to the land of our ancestors—

It would have been enough!

Had God returned us to the land of our ancestors and not summoned us to perfect this world—

It would have been enough!

*   *

How much more then, O God, must we thank You for Your boundless goodness to us!

עַל אַחַת כַּמָּה וְכַמָּה טוֹבָה כְּפוּלָה וּמְכֻפֶּלֶת לַמָּקוֹם עָלֵינוּ!

All:

For You brought us out of Egypt,
supported us in the wilderness,
gave us the Sabbath,
gave us the Torah,
brought us to the land of Israel,
sent us the prophets,
called us to be a light to the nations,
sustained us wherever
we have dwelt,
returned us to the land
of our ancestors,
and summoned us to perfect this world
    under Your unchallenged rule!

שֶׁהוֹצִיאָנוּ מִמִּצְרַיִם,
וְסִפֵּק צָרְכֵּנוּ בַּמִּדְבָּר,
וְנָתַן לָנוּ אֶת־הַשַּׁבָּת,
וְנָתַן לָנוּ אֶת־הַתּוֹרָה,
וְהִכְנִיסָנוּ לְאֶרֶץ יִשְׂרָאֵל,
וְשָׁלַח לָנוּ אֶת־הַנְּבִיאִים,
וּנְתָנָנוּ לְאוֹר גּוֹיִים,
וְהֶחֱיָנוּ בְּכָל־אַרְצוֹת
תְּפוּצָתֵנוּ,
וֶהֱשִׁיבָנוּ לְאֶרֶץ
אֲבוֹתֵינוּ,
וְצִוָּנוּ לְתַקֵּן עוֹלָם
בְּמַלְכוּת שַׁדַּי!

The cups are raised

Leader:

לְפִיכָךְ אֲנַחְנוּ חַיָּבִים לְהוֹדוֹת לְהַלֵּל לְשַׁבֵּחַ לְפָאֵר לְרוֹמֵם לְהַדֵּר לְבָרֵךְ לְעַלֵּה וּלְקַלֵּס לְמִי שֶׁעָשָׂה לַאֲבוֹתֵינוּ וְלָנוּ אֶת־ כָּל־הַנִּסִּים הָאֵלּוּ.

Therefore we thank, bless, and praise beyond measure the One who performed all these wonders for our ancestors and for us;

All:

who led us
from bondage to freedom,
from anguish to joy,
from mourning to celebration,
from darkness to light,
from subjection to redemption.

הוֹצִיאָנוּ
מֵעַבְדוּת לְחֵרוּת,
מִיָּגוֹן לְשִׂמְחָה,
מֵאֵבֶל לְיוֹם טוֹב,
וּמֵאֲפֵלָה לְאוֹר גָּדוֹל,
וּמִשִּׁעְבּוּד לִגְאֻלָּה.

Let us then sing before God
a song ever new! Halleluyah!

וְנֹאמַר לְפָנָיו
שִׁירָה חֲדָשָׁה, הַלְלוּיָהּ.

The cups are set down

*   *

THE COURAGE TO BE FREE (I)

It is by the goodness of God that in our country we have those three unspeakably precious things: freedom of speech, freedom of conscience, and the prudence never to practice either of them. (Mark Twain)

THE COURAGE TO BE FREE (II)

"But if the slave declares: 'I love my master . . . I do not wish to be freed,' his master shall take him before God. He shall be brought to the door or the doorpost, and his master shall pierce his ear with an awl; then he shall remain his slave for life (Exodus 21.56)."

Rabbi Yochanan ben Zakkai drew the following lesson: Why, of all the parts of the body, is the ear chosen for the ceremony signifying perpetual servitude? The Holy One said: "For to *Me* the people of Israel are servants (Leviticus 25.55)"—and not servants of servants! This man heard God call him to freedom, and yet he went and sought out a master: let his ear be pierced! (Talmud)

THE COURAGE TO BE FREE (III)

"The dove came back to him toward evening, and there in her bill was a plucked-off olive leaf!" (Genesis 8.11)

Where did she get it? Rabbi Bebai said: The gates of the Garden of Eden opened; she brought it out of there. Rabbi Aibo said: If she were coming from the Garden of Eden, she would have brought something more exotic, like cinnamon or balsam. But the point of the story is not where she came from but what she brought: the olive leaf was a sign to Noah, saying: "Noah, better this bitter thing from the hand of the Holy One, than a sweet thing from *your* hand." (Midrash)

Hallel, First Part

הלל, חלק ראשון

Psalm 113

הַלְלוּיָהּ!

הַלְלוּ, עַבְדֵי יְיָ, הַלְלוּ אֶת־שֵׁם יְיָ!

יְהִי שֵׁם יְיָ מְבֹרָךְ, מֵעַתָּה וְעַד עוֹלָם.

מִמִּזְרַח־שֶׁמֶשׁ עַד מְבוֹאוֹ, מְהֻלָּל שֵׁם יְיָ.

רָם עַל כָּל־גּוֹיִם יְיָ, עַל הַשָּׁמַיִם כְּבוֹדוֹ.

מִי כַּיְיָ אֱלֹהֵינוּ, הַמַּגְבִּיהִי לָשָׁבֶת,

הַמַּשְׁפִּילִי לִרְאוֹת בַּשָּׁמַיִם וּבָאָרֶץ?

מְקִימִי מֵעָפָר דָּל, מֵאַשְׁפֹּת יָרִים אֶבְיוֹן,

לְהוֹשִׁיבִי עִם נְדִיבִים, עִם נְדִיבֵי עַמּוֹ.

מוֹשִׁיבִי עֲקֶרֶת הַבַּיִת אֵם הַבָּנִים שְׂמֵחָה,

הַלְלוּיָהּ!

Halleluyah!
Sing praises, you servants of the Eternal One,
praise the name of God.

  Blessed is the name of God,
  now and forever.

From sunrise to sunset, praised be the name of God.

  Adonai is supreme above the nations;
  God's glory is higher than the heavens.

Who is like the Eternal our God
in heaven and on earth?

  Who so exalted, and yet so near:

Who raises the poor from the dust,
who lifts the wretched from the dung,

  Giving them a place among rulers,
  among the leaders of the people,

Making all who are barren,
the joyful parents of children.

  Halleluyah!

Psalm 114

בְּצֵאת יִשְׂרָאֵל מִמִּצְרָיִם, בֵּית יַעֲקֹב מֵעַם לֹעֵז,
הָיְתָה יְהוּדָה לְקָדְשׁוֹ, יִשְׂרָאֵל מַמְשְׁלוֹתָיו.
הַיָּם רָאָה וַיָּנֹס, הַיַּרְדֵּן יִסֹּב לְאָחוֹר.
הֶהָרִים רָקְדוּ כְאֵילִים, גְּבָעוֹת כִּבְנֵי־צֹאן.

מַה־לְּךָ הַיָּם, כִּי תָנוּס? הַיַּרְדֵּן, תִּסֹּב לְאָחוֹר?
הֶהָרִים, תִּרְקְדוּ כְאֵילִים? גְּבָעוֹת, כִּבְנֵי־צֹאן?
מִלִּפְנֵי אָדוֹן חוּלִי אָרֶץ, מִלִּפְנֵי אֱלוֹהַּ יַעֲקֹב,
הַהֹפְכִי הַצּוּר אֲגַם־מָיִם, חַלָּמִישׁ לְמַעְיְנוֹ־מָיִם.

When Israel went forth from Egypt, the
House of Jacob from an alien people,

    Judah became God's sanctuary,
    Israel, God's dominion.

The sea saw it and fled,
the Jordan turned back.

    The mountains skipped like rams,
    the hills like young lambs.

What ails you, O sea, that you run
away? O Jordan, that you turn back?

    O mountains, why do you skip like
    rams? Why, O hills, like young lambs?

Dance, O earth, before the Eternal;
before the God of Israel,

    Who turns the rock into a pool of
    water, the stony ground into a
    flowing spring.

*   *

p. 102

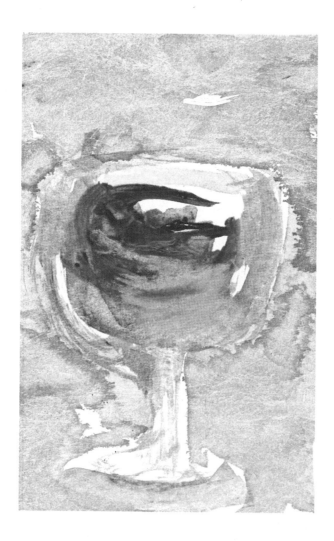

Leader:

We raise our cups in remembrance of the second promise of redemption, as it is said:

וְהִצַּלְתִּי אֶתְכֶם מֵעֲבֹדָתָם.   V'HITSALTI et-chem mei-avodatam.

I will DELIVER YOU from their bondage.

Leader:

בָּרוּךְ אַתָּה יְיָ, אֱלֹהֵינוּ מֶלֶךְ הָעוֹלָם, אֲשֶׁר גְּאָלָנוּ וְגָאַל אֶת־
אֲבוֹתֵינוּ מִמִּצְרַיִם, וְהִגִּיעָנוּ לַלַּיְלָה הַזֶּה, לֶאֱכָל־בּוֹ מַצָּה
וּמָרוֹר. כֵּן, יְיָ אֱלֹהֵינוּ וֵאלֹהֵי אֲבוֹתֵינוּ, הַגִּיעֵנוּ לְמוֹעֲדִים
וְלִרְגָלִים אֲחֵרִים, הַבָּאִים לִקְרָאתֵנוּ לְשָׁלוֹם, שְׂמֵחִים בְּבִנְיַן
עִירֶךָ, וְשָׂשִׂים בַּעֲבוֹדָתֶךָ. וְנוֹדֶה־לְךָ שִׁיר חָדָשׁ עַל גְּאֻלָּתֵנוּ
וְעַל פְּדוּת נַפְשֵׁנוּ. בָּרוּךְ אַתָּה יְיָ, גָּאַל יִשְׂרָאֵל.

We praise You, Eternal God, Ruler of the world. You
have redeemed us and our ancestors from Egypt and
enabled us to celebrate our freedom this night with
Matzah and Maror. Our God and God of all generations, be with us on all our holy and festive days; may
they find us living in peace, building Your City in
gladness, and serving You in joy. Then shall we sing to
You a new song of thanks, for the deliverance of the
world from oppression and the redemption of the spirit
from darkness. We praise You, the Eternal God,
Redeemer of Israel.

All:

בָּרוּךְ אַתָּה יְיָ, אֱלֹהֵינוּ   Baruch ata Adonai, Eloheinu
מֶלֶךְ הָעוֹלָם, בּוֹרֵא פְּרִי   melech ha-olam, borei p'ri
הַגָּפֶן.   hagafen.

We praise You, Eternal God, Ruler of time and space, Creator of
the fruit of the vine.

All now drink the second cup

*   *

47

The Meal

הסעודה

טעמי המנהגים

EXPLANATION OF THE CUSTOMS

מוציא מצה-מרור-כורך MOTSI MATZAH-MAROR-KORECH

Leader:

רַבָּן גַּמְלִיאֵל הָיָה אוֹמֵר: כָּל-שֶׁלֹּא אָמַר שְׁלֹשָׁה דְבָרִים אֵלּוּ
בַּפֶּסַח לֹא יָצָא יְדֵי חוֹבָתוֹ, וְאֵלּוּ הֵן: פֶּסַח, מַצָּה, וּמָרוֹר.

Rabban Gamaliel used to say: If, on Passover, you do
not explain these three things, you have not fulfilled
your obligation: Pesach, the Paschal lamb; Matzah, the
unleavened bread; and Maror, the bitter herbs.

Leader:

פֶּסַח שֶׁהָיוּ אֲבוֹתֵינוּ אוֹכְלִין בִּזְמַן שֶׁבֵּית הַמִּקְדָשׁ קַיָּם: עַל
שׁוּם מָה?

Pesach: Why did our ancestors eat the Passover
offering when the Temple still stood?

A Reader:

עַל שׁוּם שֶׁפָּסַח הַקָּדוֹשׁ בָּרוּךְ הוּא עַל בָּתֵּי אֲבוֹתֵינוּ
בְּמִצְרַיִם, שֶׁנֶּאֱמַר: "וַאֲמַרְתֶּם זֶבַח פֶּסַח הוּא לַיָי, אֲשֶׁר
פָּסַח עַל בָּתֵּי בְנֵי יִשְׂרָאֵל בְּמִצְרַיִם, בְּנָגְפּוֹ אֶת-
מִצְרַיִם וְאֶת-בָּתֵּינוּ הִצִּיל."

Because the Holy One passed over the houses of our
ancestors in Egypt. As it is said: "It is a Passover
offering to Adonai, the Eternal One, who passed over
the houses of the people of Israel when Egypt was
smitten; but our houses were spared."

"When the Temple still stood"—nearly two thousand years have passed since that time. But this night past and present merge, and we remember our beginnings. This bone helps us recall the Paschal Lamb our ancestors offered long ago.

The leader holds up the roasted egg and says:

This egg reminds us of the Festival Offering through which the priests, in Temple days, expressed their prayer for the well-being of the people. It is also a sign of rebirth. As all around us nature dances with new life, so may this season stir within us new strength, new hope, new joy.

Matzah:
Why do we eat it?

מַצָּה זוֹ שֶׁאָנוּ אוֹכְלִים:
עַל שׁוּם מָה?

A Reader:

עַל שׁוּם שֶׁלֹּא הִסְפִּיק בְּצֵקָם שֶׁל אֲבוֹתֵינוּ לְהַחֲמִיץ עַד
שֶׁנִּגְלָה עֲלֵיהֶם מֶלֶךְ מַלְכֵי הַמְּלָכִים, הַקָּדוֹשׁ בָּרוּךְ הוּא,
וּגְאָלָם, שֶׁנֶּאֱמַר: "וַיֹּאפוּ אֶת־הַבָּצֵק אֲשֶׁר הוֹצִיאוּ מִמִּצְרַיִם,
עֻגֹת מַצּוֹת כִּי לֹא חָמֵץ; כִּי גֹרְשׁוּ מִמִּצְרַיִם, וְלֹא יָכְלוּ
לְהִתְמַהְמֵהַּ, וְגַם צֵדָה לֹא עָשׂוּ לָהֶם."

Because the Holy One stood revealed before our ancestors to redeem them, even before their dough had time to ferment. As it is said: "They baked the dough they had brought out of Egypt into unleavened cakes, for they were driven out of Egypt without being given time to prepare food."

Leader:

Free Romans at their banquets would recline on couches, leaning to the left, to leave their right hands unencumbered, while slaves attended them. Now we re-enact that scene, *without* slaves, to celebrate the fall of slavemasters who thought their rule would last forever. So leaning is a way of rejoicing in liberation, and a symbol of our hope that before long, all the families, tribes, and peoples of the earth will eat and drink at freedom's banquet.

בָּרוּךְ אַתָּה יְיָ, אֱלֹהֵינוּ
מֶלֶךְ הָעוֹלָם, הַמּוֹצִיא לֶחֶם
מִן הָאָרֶץ.

Baruch ata Adonai, Eloheinu
melech ha-olam, hamotsi lechem
min ha-arets.

בָּרוּךְ אַתָּה יְיָ, אֱלֹהֵינוּ
מֶלֶךְ הָעוֹלָם, אֲשֶׁר קִדְּשָׁנוּ
בְּמִצְוֹתָיו וְצִוָּנוּ עַל אֲכִילַת
מַצָּה.

Baruch ata Adonai, Eloheinu
melech ha-olam, asher kid'shanu
b'mitsvotav v'tsivanu al achilat
Matzah.

We praise You, Eternal God, Ruler of time and space, for bringing forth bread from the earth.

We praise You, Eternal God, Ruler of time and space, for You hallow us with Your Mitzvot, and call us to eat unleavened bread.

All lean to the left and eat a piece of Matzah, the leader breaking a piece from the upper Matzah and another from the remainder of the middle one, and eating them together.

Leader:

Maror:
Why do we eat it?

מָרוֹר זֶה שֶׁאָנוּ אוֹכְלִים:
עַל שׁוּם מָה?

A Reader:

עַל שׁוּם שֶׁמֵּרְרוּ הַמִּצְרִים אֶת־חַיֵּי אֲבוֹתֵינוּ בְּמִצְרַיִם,
שֶׁנֶּאֱמַר: "וַיְמָרְרוּ אֶת־חַיֵּיהֶם בַּעֲבֹדָה קָשָׁה, בְּחֹמֶר
וּבִלְבֵנִים, וּבְכָל־עֲבֹדָה בַּשָּׂדֶה; אֵת כָּל־עֲבֹדָתָם אֲשֶׁר עָבְדוּ
בָהֶם בְּפָרֶךְ."

Because the Egyptians embittered the lives of our ancestors in Egypt. As it is said: "They made life bitter for them with hard labor at mortar and brick, and with every kind of field work; they drove them in their work with utter ruthlessness."

Leader:

Before eating the Maror, we dip it in Charoset. It looks like the clay and straw with which our people were forced to make bricks for Pharaoh's building projects in Egypt. Its sweet taste softens, but does not remove, the bitter memory of their slavery.

All take a piece of Maror, dip it in Charoset,
and say:

בָּרוּךְ אַתָּה יְיָ, אֱלֹהֵינוּ
מֶלֶךְ הָעוֹלָם, אֲשֶׁר קִדְּשָׁנוּ
בְּמִצְוֹתָיו וְצִוָּנוּ עַל אֲכִילַת
מָרוֹר.

Baruch ata Adonai, Eloheinu
melech ha-olam, asher kid'shanu
b'mitsvotav v'tsivanu al achilat
Maror.

We praise You, Eternal God, Ruler of time and space, for You
hallow us with Your Mitzvot, and call us to eat bitter herbs.

The Maror is eaten

All place another piece of Maror and Charoset between
two pieces of Matzah, the leader breaking these
from the lower Matzah. All recite:

כֵּן עָשָׂה הִלֵּל בִּזְמַן שֶׁבֵּית הַמִּקְדָּשׁ הָיָה קַיָּם: הָיָה כּוֹרֵךְ
מַצָּה וּמָרוֹר וְאוֹכֵל בְּיַחַד, לְקַיֵּם מַה־שֶׁנֶּאֱמַר: "עַל מַצּוֹת
וּמְרֹרִים יֹאכְלֻהוּ."

This was Hillel's practice in the days of the Temple: he
would combine (the Passover lamb with) unleavened
bread and bitter herbs (Pesach, Matzah, Maror) and eat
them together, to fulfill the verse: "They shall eat it
with unleavened bread and bitter herbs."

Leader:

We hold the Matzah of freedom, the 'mortar' of forced labor, the
bitter Maror of bondage. We take into ourselves the joys and
sorrows of the ages.

All now eat the 'Hillel Sandwich'

*   *

51

The Meal is Served   שלחן עורך

*   *

Tsafun   צפון

> At the conclusion of the meal the Afikoman is eaten. Thus, as promised earlier, the lost is found, the hidden revealed, the broken made whole. The children seek and find the Afikoman toward the end of the meal, or the leader seeks *and fails* to find it. In either case, it is eventually 'found' by the children, who receive a reward for their efforts. The meal ends with the eating of the Matzah of the Afikoman.

*   *

Before the Afikoman is eaten the leader might say:

This Matzah is called צָפוּן, tsafun, that which was 'hidden' or 'stored up'. So we pray to the God of our ancestors and God of our descendants: May the time come when the lost will be found, the broken made whole, the hidden revealed. As it is said:

How great is the goodness You have	מָה רַב טוּבְךָ
stored up for those who	אֲשֶׁר צָפַנְתָ
revere You! (Psalm 31.20)	לִירֵאֶיךָ!

*   *

Thanksgiving for the Meal

בָּרֵךְ

The cups are re-filled

A short form of Thanksgiving begins on page 58.

Psalm 126

All:

שִׁיר הַמַּעֲלוֹת בְּשׁוּב יְיָ אֶת־שִׁיבַת צִיּוֹן הָיִינוּ כְּחֹלְמִים. אָז יִמָּלֵא שְׂחוֹק פִּינוּ וּלְשׁוֹנֵנוּ רִנָּה. אָז יֹאמְרוּ בַגּוֹיִם הִגְדִּיל יְיָ לַעֲשׂוֹת עִם אֵלֶּה. הִגְדִּיל יְיָ לַעֲשׂוֹת עִמָּנוּ הָיִינוּ שְׂמֵחִים. שׁוּבָה יְיָ אֶת־שְׁבִיתֵנוּ כַּאֲפִיקִים בַּנֶּגֶב. הַזֹּרְעִים בְּדִמְעָה בְּרִנָּה יִקְצֹרוּ. הָלוֹךְ יֵלֵךְ וּבָכֹה נֹשֵׂא מֶשֶׁךְ הַזָּרַע, בֹּא יָבֹא בְרִנָּה נֹשֵׂא אֲלֻמֹּתָיו.

*   *

Leader:

רַבּוֹתַי נְבָרֵךְ.

All:

יְהִי שֵׁם יְיָ מְבֹרָךְ מֵעַתָּה וְעַד עוֹלָם.

Leader:

בִּרְשׁוּת רַבּוֹתַי, נְבָרֵךְ אֱלֹהֵינוּ שֶׁאָכַלְנוּ מִשֶּׁלּוֹ.

All:

בָּרוּךְ אֱלֹהֵינוּ שֶׁאָכַלְנוּ מִשֶּׁלּוֹ וּבְטוּבוֹ חָיִינוּ.

Leader:

בָּרוּךְ הוּא וּבָרוּךְ שְׁמוֹ!

All:

בָּרוּךְ אַתָּה יְיָ, אֱלֹהֵינוּ מֶלֶךְ הָעוֹלָם, הַזָּן אֶת־הָעוֹלָם כֻּלּוֹ בְּטוּבוֹ בְּחֵן, בְּחֶסֶד וּבְרַחֲמִים. הוּא נוֹתֵן לֶחֶם לְכָל־בָּשָׂר, כִּי לְעוֹלָם חַסְדּוֹ. וּבְטוּבוֹ הַגָּדוֹל תָּמִיד לֹא חָסַר לָנוּ, וְאַל יֶחְסַר־לָנוּ מָזוֹן לְעוֹלָם וָעֶד, בַּעֲבוּר שְׁמוֹ הַגָּדוֹל. כִּי הוּא אֵל זָן וּמְפַרְנֵס לַכֹּל וּמֵטִיב לַכֹּל וּמֵכִין מָזוֹן לְכָל־בְּרִיּוֹתָיו אֲשֶׁר בָּרָא. בָּרוּךְ אַתָּה יְיָ, הַזָּן אֶת־הַכֹּל.

נוֹדֶה לְךָ, יְיָ אֱלֹהֵינוּ, עַל שֶׁהִנְחַלְתָּ לַאֲבוֹתֵינוּ אֶרֶץ חֶמְדָּה
טוֹבָה וּרְחָבָה, וְעַל שֶׁהוֹצֵאתָנוּ, יְיָ אֱלֹהֵינוּ, מֵאֶרֶץ מִצְרַיִם,
וּפְדִיתָנוּ מִבֵּית עֲבָדִים, וְעַל בְּרִיתְךָ שֶׁחָתַמְתָּ בִּלְבָבֵנוּ, וְעַל
תּוֹרָתְךָ שֶׁלִּמַּדְתָּנוּ, וְעַל חֻקֶּיךָ שֶׁהוֹדַעְתָּנוּ, וְעַל חַיִּים, חֵן
וָחֶסֶד שֶׁחוֹנַנְתָּנוּ, וְעַל אֲכִילַת מָזוֹן שֶׁאַתָּה זָן וּמְפַרְנֵס
אוֹתָנוּ תָּמִיד, בְּכָל־יוֹם וּבְכָל־עֵת וּבְכָל־שָׁעָה.

וְעַל הַכֹּל, יְיָ אֱלֹהֵינוּ, אֲנַחְנוּ מוֹדִים לָךְ וּמְבָרְכִים אוֹתָךְ.
יִתְבָּרַךְ שִׁמְךָ בְּפִי כָּל־חַי תָּמִיד לְעוֹלָם וָעֶד, כַּכָּתוּב:

All:

וְאָכַלְתָּ וְשָׂבָעְתָּ וּבֵרַכְתָּ אֶת־יְיָ אֱלֹהֶיךָ עַל הָאָרֶץ הַטּוֹבָה
אֲשֶׁר נָתַן לָךְ. בָּרוּךְ אַתָּה יְיָ, עַל הָאָרֶץ וְעַל הַמָּזוֹן.

Leader:

אֱלֹהֵינוּ אָבִינוּ, רְעֵנוּ זוּנֵנוּ, פַּרְנְסֵנוּ וְכַלְכְּלֵנוּ וְהַרְוִיחֵנוּ,
וְהַרְוַח־לָנוּ, יְיָ אֱלֹהֵינוּ, מְהֵרָה מִכָּל־צָרוֹתֵינוּ. וְנָא אַל
תַּצְרִיכֵנוּ, יְיָ אֱלֹהֵינוּ, לֹא לִידֵי מַתְּנַת בָּשָׂר וָדָם וְלֹא לִידֵי
הַלְוָאָתָם, כִּי אִם לְיָדְךָ הַמְּלֵאָה הַפְּתוּחָה הַגְּדוּשָׁה
וְהָרְחָבָה, שֶׁלֹּא נֵבוֹשׁ וְלֹא נִכָּלֵם לְעוֹלָם וָעֶד.

On Shabbat

Leader:

רְצֵה וְהַחֲלִיצֵנוּ, יְיָ אֱלֹהֵינוּ, בְּמִצְוֹתֶיךָ וּבְמִצְוַת יוֹם הַשְּׁבִיעִי
הַשַּׁבָּת הַגָּדוֹל וְהַקָּדוֹשׁ הַזֶּה, לִשְׁבָּת־בּוֹ וְלָנוּחַ בּוֹ בְּאַהֲבָה
כְּמִצְוַת רְצוֹנֶךָ. בִּרְצוֹנְךָ הָנַח לָנוּ, יְיָ אֱלֹהֵינוּ, שֶׁלֹּא תְהִי צָרָה
וְיָגוֹן וַאֲנָחָה בְּיוֹם מְנוּחָתֵנוּ, וְהַרְאֵנוּ יְיָ אֱלֹהֵינוּ בְּנֶחָמַת
יִשְׂרָאֵל עַמֶּךָ, וּבְבִנְיַן יְרוּשָׁלַיִם עִיר קָדְשֶׁךָ, כִּי אַתָּה הוּא
בַּעַל הַיְשׁוּעוֹת וּבַעַל הַנֶּחָמוֹת.

אֱלֹהֵינוּ וֵאלֹהֵי אֲבוֹתֵינוּ, יַעֲלֶה וְיָבֹא וְיַגִּיעַ וְיֵרָאֶה וְיֵרָצֶה וְיִשָּׁמַע וְיִפָּקֵד וְיִזָּכֵר זִכְרוֹנֵנוּ וְזִכְרוֹן כָּל־עַמְּךָ בֵּית יִשְׂרָאֵל לְפָנֶיךָ, לְטוֹבָה לְחֵן לְחֶסֶד וּלְרַחֲמִים, לְחַיִּים וּלְשָׁלוֹם בְּיוֹם חַג הַמַּצּוֹת הַזֶּה. זָכְרֵנוּ יְיָ אֱלֹהֵינוּ בּוֹ לְטוֹבָה, וּפָקְדֵנוּ בוֹ לִבְרָכָה, וְהוֹשִׁיעֵנוּ בוֹ לְחַיִּים. וּבִדְבַר יְשׁוּעָה וְרַחֲמִים חוּס וְחָנֵּנוּ, וְרַחֵם עָלֵינוּ וְהוֹשִׁיעֵנוּ כִּי אֵלֶיךָ עֵינֵינוּ, כִּי אֵל חַנּוּן וְרַחוּם אָתָּה.

וּבְנֵה יְרוּשָׁלַיִם עִיר הַקֹּדֶשׁ בִּמְהֵרָה בְיָמֵינוּ. בָּרוּךְ אַתָּה, יְיָ, בּוֹנֵה בְרַחֲמָיו יְרוּשָׁלָיִם. אָמֵן.

בָּרוּךְ אַתָּה, יְיָ אֱלֹהֵינוּ, מֶלֶךְ הָעוֹלָם, הָאֵל אָבִינוּ מַלְכֵּנוּ אַדִּירֵנוּ בּוֹרְאֵנוּ גּוֹאֲלֵנוּ יוֹצְרֵנוּ קְדוֹשֵׁנוּ קְדוֹשׁ יַעֲקֹב, רוֹעֵנוּ רוֹעֵה יִשְׂרָאֵל, הַמֶּלֶךְ הַטּוֹב וְהַמֵּטִיב לַכֹּל, שֶׁבְּכָל־יוֹם וָיוֹם הוּא הֵטִיב, הוּא מֵטִיב, הוּא יֵיטִיב לָנוּ. הוּא גְמָלָנוּ הוּא גוֹמְלֵנוּ הוּא יִגְמְלֵנוּ לָעַד, לְחֵן לְחֶסֶד וּלְרַחֲמִים וּלְרֶוַח, הַצָּלָה וְהַצְלָחָה, בְּרָכָה וִישׁוּעָה, נֶחָמָה, פַּרְנָסָה וְכַלְכָּלָה וְרַחֲמִים וְחַיִּים וְשָׁלוֹם וְכָל־טוֹב, וּמִכָּל־טוּב אַל יְחַסְּרֵנוּ.

הָרַחֲמָן, הוּא יִמְלֹךְ עָלֵינוּ לְעוֹלָם וָעֶד.

הָרַחֲמָן, הוּא יִתְבָּרַךְ בַּשָּׁמַיִם וּבָאָרֶץ.

הָרַחֲמָן, הוּא יִשְׁתַּבַּח לְדוֹר דּוֹרִים, וְיִתְפָּאַר־בָּנוּ לָעַד וּלְנֵצַח נְצָחִים, וְיִתְהַדַּר־בָּנוּ לָעַד וּלְעוֹלְמֵי עוֹלָמִים.

הָרַחֲמָן, הוּא יִשְׁלַח בְּרָכָה מְרֻבָּה בַּבַּיִת הַזֶּה, וְעַל שֻׁלְחָן זֶה שֶׁאָכַלְנוּ עָלָיו.

הָרַחֲמָן, הוּא יִשְׁלַח־לָנוּ אֶת־אֵלִיָּהוּ הַנָּבִיא, זָכוּר לַטּוֹב, וִיבַשֶּׂר־לָנוּ בְּשׂוֹרוֹת טוֹבוֹת יְשׁוּעוֹת וְנֶחָמוֹת.

הָרַחֲמָן, הוּא יְבָרֵךְ אוֹתָנוּ וְאֶת־כָּל־אֲשֶׁר לָנוּ, כְּמוֹ שֶׁנִּתְבָּרְכוּ אֲבוֹתֵינוּ אַבְרָהָם יִצְחָק וְיַעֲקֹב בַּכֹּל מִכֹּל כֹּל, כֵּן יְבָרֵךְ אוֹתָנוּ כֻּלָּנוּ יַחַד בִּבְרָכָה שְׁלֵמָה, וְנֹאמַר: אָמֵן.

All:

וְנִשָּׂא בְרָכָה מֵאֵת יְיָ, וּצְדָקָה מֵאֱלֹהֵי יִשְׁעֵנוּ, וְנִמְצָא־חֵן וְשֵׂכֶל טוֹב בְּעֵינֵי אֱלֹהִים וְאָדָם.

On Shabbat

Leader:

הָרַחֲמָן, הוּא יַנְחִילֵנוּ יוֹם שֶׁכֻּלּוֹ שַׁבָּת.

Leader:

הָרַחֲמָן, הוּא יַנְחִילֵנוּ יוֹם שֶׁכֻּלּוֹ טוֹב.

הָרַחֲמָן, הוּא יְזַכֵּנוּ לִימוֹת הַמָּשִׁיחַ וּלְחַיֵּי הָעוֹלָם הַבָּא.

All:

עֹשֶׂה שָׁלוֹם בִּמְרוֹמָיו, הוּא יַעֲשֶׂה שָׁלוֹם עָלֵינוּ וְעַל כָּל־יִשְׂרָאֵל, וְאִמְרוּ אָמֵן.

יְיָ עֹז לְעַמּוֹ יִתֵּן, יְיָ יְבָרֵךְ אֶת־עַמּוֹ בַשָּׁלוֹם.

Continue on page 62.

Thanksgiving for the Meal, Short Form ברך, בקצור

The cups are refilled.

Psalm 126

שִׁיר הַמַּעֲלוֹת.	Shir Hama'alot.
בְּשׁוּב יְיָ אֶת־שִׁיבַת צִיּוֹן	B'shuv Adonai et shivat Tsi-yon
הָיִינוּ כְּחֹלְמִים.	Hayinu k'cholmim.
אָז יִמָּלֵא שְׂחוֹק פִּינוּ	Az yimalei s'chok pinu
וּלְשׁוֹנֵנוּ רִנָּה.	u-l'shoneinu rina.
אָז יֹאמְרוּ בַגּוֹיִם,	Az yom'ru va-go-yim,
הִגְדִּיל יְיָ לַעֲשׂוֹת עִם אֵלֶּה.	Higdil Adonai la'asot im eileh.
הִגְדִּיל יְיָ לַעֲשׂוֹת עִמָּנוּ,	Higdil Adonai la'asot imanu,
הָיִינוּ שְׂמֵחִים.	ha-yinu s'meichim.
שׁוּבָה יְיָ אֶת־שְׁבִיתֵנוּ	Shuva Adonai et sh'viteinu
כַּאֲפִיקִים בַּנֶּגֶב.	ka'afikim banegev.
הַזֹּרְעִים בְּדִמְעָה בְּרִנָּה יִקְצֹרוּ.	Hazor'im b'dim-ah b'rina yik-tsoru.
הָלוֹךְ יֵלֵךְ וּבָכֹה,	Haloch yeileich u-vacho,
נֹשֵׂא מֶשֶׁךְ הַזָּרַע,	nosei meshech hazara,
בֹּא יָבֹא בְרִנָּה נֹשֵׂא אֲלֻמֹּתָיו.	bo yavo v'rina nosei alumotav.

A Song of Ascents.

When God restores the exiles of Zion, it shall seem like a dream. Our mouths shall be filled with laughter, our tongues with joyful song. Then they shall say among the nations: "God has done great things for them." Yes, God has done great things for us, and we rejoice. Eternal God, restore our fortunes, as streams revive the desert. Then those who sow in tears shall reap in joy. Then those who go forth weeping, bearing their seeds, shall come home with shouts of joy, bearing their sheaves.

*   *

Leader:

בִּרְשׁוּת רַבּוֹתַי,	Bir'shut rabotai,
נְבָרֵךְ אֱלֹהֵינוּ שֶׁאָכַלְנוּ	n'vareich Eloheinu sheh-achalnu
מִשֶּׁלוֹ.	mishelo.

בָּרוּךְ אֱלֹהֵינוּ שֶׁאָכַלְנוּ
מִשֶׁלוֹ, וּבְטוּבוֹ חָיִינוּ.

Baruch Eloheinu sheh-achalnu
mishelo, u-v'tuvo cha-yinu.

בָּרוּךְ אַתָּה יְיָ, אֱלֹהֵינוּ מֶלֶךְ
הָעוֹלָם, הַזָּן אֶת־הָעוֹלָם כֻּלוֹ
בְּטוּבוֹ, בְּחֵן בְּחֶסֶד וּבְרַחֲמִים
הוּא נוֹתֵן לֶחֶם לְכָל־בָּשָׂר, כִּי
לְעוֹלָם חַסְדּוֹ. וּבְטוּבוֹ הַגָּדוֹל
תָּמִיד לֹא חָסַר לָנוּ, וְאַל יֶחְסַר־
לָנוּ מָזוֹן לְעוֹלָם וָעֶד, בַּעֲבוּר
שְׁמוֹ הַגָּדוֹל. כִּי הוּא אֵל זָן
וּמְפַרְנֵס לַכֹּל וּמֵטִיב לַכֹּל
וּמֵכִין מָזוֹן לְכָל־בְּרִיּוֹתָיו
אֲשֶׁר בָּרָא. בָּרוּךְ אַתָּה יְיָ,
הַזָּן אֶת־הַכֹּל.

Baruch ata Adonai, Eloheinu melech
ha-olam, hazan et ha-olam kulo
b'tuvo, b'chein b'chesed u-v'rachamim
hu notein lechem l'chol basar, ki
l'olam chasdo. U-v'tuvo hagadol
tamid lo chasar lanu, v'al yechsar
lanu mazon l'olam va-ed, ba-avur
sh'mo ha-gadol. Ki hu Eil zan
u-m'farneis lakol u-meitiv lakol
u-meichin mazon l'chol b'ri-yotav
asher bara. Baruch ata Adonai,
hazan et hakol.

We praise You, Eternal God, Ruler of time and space, whose
goodness sustains the world. With grace, love, and compassion
You are the Source of bread for all who live, for Your love is
unending. By Your great goodness we do not lack and will not
ever lack. For You are in the goodness that sustains and nourishes
all, providing food enough for every living being. We praise You,
Eternal God, Source of food for all who live.

וּבְנֵה יְרוּשָׁלַיִם עִיר הַקֹּדֶשׁ
בִּמְהֵרָה בְיָמֵינוּ. בָּרוּךְ אַתָּה
יְיָ, בּוֹנֶה בְרַחֲמָיו
יְרוּשָׁלָיִם. אָמֵן.

U-v'nei Y'rushalayim ir ha-kodesh
bim'heira v'yameinu. Baruch ata
Adonai, boneh v'rachamav
Y'rushalayim. *Amen*

Let Jerusalem, the City of Holiness, be built in our time. We praise
You, Eternal God, who in compassion will build Jerusalem. Amen.

On Shabbat

Leader:

הָרַחֲמָן, הוּא יַנְחִילֵנוּ יוֹם
שֶׁכֻּלוֹ שַׁבָּת.

Harachaman, hu yanchileinu yom
sheh-kulo Shabbat.

Merciful One: bring us to the Day that is All Shabbat. *Amen.*

Continued on p. 62

59

Leader:

הָרַחֲמָן, הוּא יַנְחִילֵנוּ יוֹם
שֶׁכֻּלּוֹ טוֹב.

Harachaman, hu yanchileinu yom
sheh-kulo Tov.

הָרַחֲמָן, הוּא יְזַכֵּנוּ לִימוֹת
הַמָּשִׁיחַ וּלְחַיֵּי
הָעוֹלָם הַבָּא.

Harachaman, hu y'zakeinu li-mot
ha-mashi-ach u-l'chayei
ha-olam haba.

Merciful One: bring us to the Day that is All Good. *Amen.*
Merciful One: find us worthy of witnessing the time of
redemption and of attaining eternal life. *Amen.*

All:

עֹשֶׂה שָׁלוֹם בִּמְרוֹמָיו, הוּא יַעֲשֶׂה
שָׁלוֹם עָלֵינוּ וְעַל כָּל־יִשְׂרָאֵל,
וְאִמְרוּ אָמֵן.
יְיָ עֹז לְעַמּוֹ יִתֵּן, יְיָ
יְבָרֵךְ אֶת־עַמּוֹ בַשָּׁלוֹם.

Oseh shalom bim'romav, hu ya'aseh
shalom aleinu v'al kol Yisra'el,
v'im'ru amen.
Adonai oz l'amo yitein, Adonai
y'vareich et amo vashalom.

May the One who causes peace to reign in the heavens above
grant peace to us, to all Israel, and all the world.

O God, give strength unto Your people;
O God, bless Your people with peace. Amen.

The Third Cup   כוס של ברכה

Leader:

We raise our cups in remembrance of the third promise of
redemption, as it is said:

All:

וְגָאַלְתִּי אֶתְכֶם בִּזְרוֹעַ
נְטוּיָה . . .

V'GA-ALTI et-chem bizro-a
n'tuyah . . .

I will REDEEM YOU with outstretched arm . . .

62

בָּרוּךְ אַתָּה יְיָ, אֱלֹהֵינוּ מֶלֶךְ הָעוֹלָם, בּוֹרֵא פְּרִי הַגָּפֶן. Baruch ata Adonai, Eloheinu melech ha-olam, borei p'ri hagafen.

We praise You, Eternal God, Ruler of time and space, Creator of the fruit of the vine.

All now drink the third cup

*   *

The following section may be read wholly or in part

'The Cup of Elijah' begins on page 71

Hallel, Second Part

הלל, חלק שני

(The omission of Psalms 115 and 116 is explained in the Notes)

Psalm 117

הַלְלוּ אֶת־יְיָ, כָּל־גּוֹיִם, שַׁבְּחוּהוּ, כָּל־הָאֻמִּים.
כִּי גָבַר עָלֵינוּ חַסְדּוֹ, וֶאֱמֶת יְיָ לְעוֹלָם.
הַלְלוּיָהּ.

Praise the Eternal One, all you nations!
    Extol God, all you peoples!
God's love for us is tremendous;
    The Divine faithfulness is everlasting.
Halleluyah!

From Psalm 118

הוֹדוּ לַיְיָ כִּי־טוֹב, כִּי לְעוֹלָם חַסְדּוֹ.
יֹאמַר־נָא יִשְׂרָאֵל, כִּי לְעוֹלָם חַסְדּוֹ.
יֹאמְרוּ־נָא בֵית אַהֲרֹן, כִּי לְעוֹלָם חַסְדּוֹ.
יֹאמְרוּ־נָא יִרְאֵי יְיָ, כִּי לְעוֹלָם חַסְדּוֹ.

מִן הַמֵּצַר קָרָאתִי יָּהּ; עָנָנִי בַמֶּרְחָב יָהּ.
יְיָ לִי, לֹא אִירָא; מַה־יַּעֲשֶׂה לִי אָדָם?

יְיָ לִי בְּעֹזְרָי, וַאֲנִי אֶרְאֶה בְשׂנְאָי.

טוֹב לַחֲסוֹת בַּיְיָ מִבְּטֹחַ בָּאָדָם.
טוֹב לַחֲסוֹת בַּיְיָ מִבְּטֹחַ בִּנְדִיבִים.

עָזִּי וְזִמְרָת יָהּ, וַיְהִי־לִי לִישׁוּעָה.
קוֹל רִנָּה וִישׁוּעָה בְּאָהֳלֵי צַדִּיקִים:
יְמִין יְיָ עֹשָׂה חָיִל!
יְמִין יְיָ רוֹמֵמָה, יְמִין יְיָ עֹשָׂה חָיִל!

לֹא אָמוּת כִּי אֶחְיֶה, וַאֲסַפֵּר מַעֲשֵׂי יָהּ.
פִּתְחוּ־לִי שַׁעֲרֵי־צֶדֶק; אָבֹא־בָם, אוֹדֶה יָהּ.

64

זֶה־הַשַּׁעַר לַיְיָ, צַדִּיקִים יָבֹאוּ בוֹ.
אוֹדְךָ כִּי עֲנִיתָנִי, וַתְּהִי־לִי לִישׁוּעָה.

אֶבֶן מָאֲסוּ הַבּוֹנִים, הָיְתָה לְרֹאשׁ פִּנָּה.
מֵאֵת יְיָ הָיְתָה זֹּאת; הִיא נִפְלָאת בְּעֵינֵינוּ.

זֶה הַיּוֹם עָשָׂה יְיָ, נָגִילָה וְנִשְׂמְחָה בוֹ.

אָנָּא יְיָ, הוֹשִׁיעָה נָּא!
אָנָּא יְיָ, הוֹשִׁיעָה נָּא!

אָנָּא יְיָ, הַצְלִיחָה נָּא!
אָנָּא יְיָ, הַצְלִיחָה נָּא!

בָּרוּךְ הַבָּא בְּשֵׁם יְיָ, בֵּרַכְנוּכֶם מִבֵּית יְיָ.

אֵלִי אַתָּה וְאוֹדֶךָּ, אֱלֹהַי אֲרוֹמְמֶךָּ.

הוֹדוּ לַיְיָ כִּי טוֹב, כִּי לְעוֹלָם חַסְדּוֹ.

Give thanks to God, who is good,
whose love is everlasting.

    Let Israel now say:
    God's love is everlasting.

Let the House of Aaron now say:
God's love is everlasting.

    Let all who fear God now say:
    God's love is everlasting.

In distress I called to the Most High,
who answered me and set me free.

    God is with me; I shall not fear;
    what can mortals do to me?

With God as my Helper,
I can face any foe.

    It is better to trust God
    than to rely on mortals.

It is better to trust in God
than to rely on the mighty.

The Eternal One, my strength and my shield,
has become my deliverance.

Hear! Glad songs of triumph in
the tents of the righteous!
God's hand does wonders!

God's hand is raised high!
God's hand does wonders!

I shall not die, but live
to tell God's deeds.

Open for me the gates of righteousness;
let me enter them and give thanks to God.

This is the gate of the Eternal;
the righteous shall enter it.

I thank You, for You have answered me,
and have been my salvation.

The stone the builders rejected
has become the chief cornerstone.

This is the Eternal's doing;
it is marvellous in our eyes.

This is the day that God has made;
let us rejoice and be glad in it.

Eternal God, save us!
Eternal God, save us!

Eternal God, prosper us!
Eternal God, prosper us!

Blessed is the one who comes in God's name;
here, in God's house, may you be blessed.

You are my God, and I thank You;
You are my God, I exalt You.

Give thanks to God, who is good,
whose love is everlasting.

*   *

יְהַלְלוּךָ, יְיָ אֱלֹהֵינוּ, כָּל־מַעֲשֶׂיךָ, וַחֲסִידֶיךָ צַדִּיקִים עוֹשֵׂי
רְצוֹנֶךָ, וְכָל־עַמְּךָ בֵּית יִשְׂרָאֵל, בְּרִנָּה יוֹדוּ וִיבָרְכוּ, וִישַׁבְּחוּ
וִיפָאֲרוּ, וִירוֹמְמוּ וְיַעֲרִיצוּ, וְיַקְדִּישׁוּ וְיַמְלִיכוּ אֶת־שִׁמְךָ,
מַלְכֵּנוּ. כִּי לְךָ טוֹב לְהוֹדוֹת, וּלְשִׁמְךָ נָאֶה לְזַמֵּר, כִּי מֵעוֹלָם
וְעַד עוֹלָם אַתָּה אֵל.

בָּרוּךְ אַתָּה יְיָ, מֶלֶךְ מְהֻלָּל בַּתִּשְׁבָּחוֹת.

נִשְׁמַת כָּל־חַי תְּבָרֵךְ אֶת־שִׁמְךָ, יְיָ אֱלֹהֵינוּ, וְרוּחַ כָּל־בָּשָׂר
תְּפָאֵר וּתְרוֹמֵם זִכְרְךָ מַלְכֵּנוּ תָּמִיד. מִן הָעוֹלָם וְעַד הָעוֹלָם
אַתָּה אֵל, וּמִבַּלְעָדֶיךָ אֵין לָנוּ מֶלֶךְ גּוֹאֵל וּמוֹשִׁיעַ, פּוֹדֶה
וּמַצִּיל וּמְפַרְנֵס וּמְרַחֵם בְּכָל־עֵת צָרָה וְצוּקָה, אֵין לָנוּ מֶלֶךְ
אֶלָּא אָתָּה.

אֱלֹהֵי הָרִאשׁוֹנִים וְהָאַחֲרוֹנִים, אֱלוֹהַּ כָּל־בְּרִיּוֹת, אֲדוֹן כָּל־
תּוֹלָדוֹת, הַמְהֻלָּל בְּרֹב הַתִּשְׁבָּחוֹת, הַמְנַהֵג עוֹלָמוֹ בְּחֶסֶד
וּבְרִיּוֹתָיו בְּרַחֲמִים.

וַייָ לֹא יָנוּם וְלֹא יִישָׁן, הַמְעוֹרֵר יְשֵׁנִים וְהַמֵּקִיץ נִרְדָּמִים
וְהַמֵּשִׂיחַ אִלְּמִים וְהַמַּתִּיר אֲסוּרִים וְהַסּוֹמֵךְ נוֹפְלִים וְהַזּוֹקֵף
כְּפוּפִים. לְךָ לְבַדְּךָ אֲנַחְנוּ מוֹדִים.

אִלּוּ פִינוּ מָלֵא שִׁירָה כַּיָּם
וּלְשׁוֹנֵנוּ רִנָּה כַּהֲמוֹן גַּלָּיו
וְשִׂפְתוֹתֵינוּ שֶׁבַח כְּמֶרְחֲבֵי רָקִיעַ
וְעֵינֵינוּ מְאִירוֹת כַּשֶּׁמֶשׁ וְכַיָּרֵחַ
וְיָדֵינוּ פְרוּשׂוֹת כְּנִשְׁרֵי שָׁמָיִם
וְרַגְלֵינוּ קַלּוֹת כָּאַיָּלוֹת
אֵין אֲנַחְנוּ מַסְפִּיקִים לְהוֹדוֹת לְךָ, יְיָ אֱלֹהֵינוּ וֵאלֹהֵי
אֲבוֹתֵינוּ, וּלְבָרֵךְ אֶת־שִׁמְךָ עַל אַחַת מֵאָלֶף אֶלֶף אַלְפֵי
אֲלָפִים וְרִבֵּי רְבָבוֹת פְּעָמִים הַטּוֹבוֹת שֶׁעָשִׂיתָ עִם אֲבוֹתֵינוּ
וְעִמָּנוּ.

מִמִּצְרַיִם גְּאַלְתָּנוּ, יְיָ אֱלֹהֵינוּ, וּמִבֵּית עֲבָדִים פְּדִיתָנוּ, בְּרָעָב
זַנְתָּנוּ וּבְשָׂבָע כִּלְכַּלְתָּנוּ, מֵחֶרֶב הִצַּלְתָּנוּ וּמִדֶּבֶר מִלַּטְתָּנוּ,
וּמֵחֳלָיִים רָעִים וְנֶאֱמָנִים דִּלִּיתָנוּ. עַד הֵנָּה עֲזָרוּנוּ רַחֲמֶיךָ
וְלֹא עֲזָבוּנוּ חֲסָדֶיךָ, יְיָ אֱלֹהֵינוּ, לָנֶצַח.

עַל כֵּן אֵבָרִים שֶׁפִּלַּגְתָּ בָּנוּ, וְרוּחַ וּנְשָׁמָה שֶׁנָּפַחְתָּ בְּאַפֵּינוּ,
וְלָשׁוֹן אֲשֶׁר שַׂמְתָּ בְּפֵינוּ, הֵן הֵם יוֹדוּ וִיבָרְכוּ וִישַׁבְּחוּ
וִיפָאֲרוּ אֶת־שִׁמְךָ, מַלְכֵּנוּ.

כִּי כָל־פֶּה לְךָ יוֹדֶה, וְכָל־לָשׁוֹן לְךָ תִשָּׁבַע, וְכָל־בֶּרֶךְ לְךָ
תִכְרַע, וְכָל־קוֹמָה לְפָנֶיךָ תִשְׁתַּחֲוֶה, וְכָל־לְבָבוֹת יִירָאוּךָ,
וְכָל־קֶרֶב וּכְלָיוֹת יְזַמְּרוּ לִשְׁמֶךָ.

כַּדָּבָר שֶׁכָּתוּב: כָּל־עַצְמוֹתַי תֹּאמַרְנָה: "יְיָ, מִי כָמוֹךָ?"
כָּאמוּר, "לְדָוִד, בָּרְכִי, נַפְשִׁי, אֶת־יְיָ, וְכָל־קְרָבַי אֶת־שֵׁם
קָדְשׁוֹ!"

*   *

Benediction of Song · ברכת השיר

Leader:

Let all creation praise You, Eternal God. Let all the faithful and
righteous, who do Your will, and the whole House of Israel, Your
people, thank, bless, extol, and exalt You in joyful song, and
proclaim Your holiness and sovereignty. For how good it is to
thank You, how pleasant to sing to You, the everlasting God!

All:

We praise You, the Sovereign God, ever extolled in song.

Leader:

Let every living soul give praise to Your name, Eternal God, and
let every human spirit acclaim Your majesty for ever.

Through all eternity You are God; we have no ruler but You, no
other helper or redeemer to sustain, uphold, and pity us in time of
trouble and danger.

All:

God of all ages, God of all creatures, Ruler of all generations, all
praise to You. You guide the world with faithful love, Your
creatures with tender mercy.

You neither slumber nor sleep; You awaken the sleeping and rouse the dormant. You give speech to the silent, freedom to the enslaved, support to the falling, justice to the oppressed. To You alone we give thanks.

Yet though our mouths should overflow with song as the sea,
our tongues with melody as the roaring waves,
our lips with praise as the heavens' wide expanse;
and though our eyes were to shine as the sun and the moon,
our arms extend like eagles' wings,
our feet speed swiftly as deer—
still we could not fully thank You,
Eternal our God, God of all ages,
or praise Your name enough,
for Your infinite kindness to our ancestors and to us.

From Egypt You redeemed us, from the house of bondage You released us. In famine time You have fed us, in times of plenty sustained us. From the sword You have delivered us, from plague have rescued us, and from dread diseases You have healed us. Your mercy has been with us to this day, and Your faithful love has never failed us; stay with us, then, O God, for ever.

And so these limbs You have formed in us,
this spirit You have breathed into us,
and this tongue You have set in our mouths
shall thank and bless You, extol and exalt You,
proclaiming Your holiness and sovereighty.

Then shall every mouth affirm You,
and every tongue give You allegiance;
every knee shall bend to You,
and every body bow down to You;
every heart shall then revere You,
and every fibre of our being
shall sing Your praise.

Leader:

For thus is it written:

"All my limbs shall say,"

'Who is like You. Eternal One?'"

Who *is* like You? Who is Your equal?

Who can compare with You,

O great, mighty, and awesome God,

God supreme,

Maker of heaven and earth?

Therefore

we praise You,

proclaim Your glory,

and bless Your holy name.

As it is said:

"Bless the Eternal, O my soul;

let all that is within me

bless God's holy name."

*   *

'FIT' TO BE FREE

A people may prefer a free government, but if, from indolence, or carelessness, or cowardice . . . they are unequal to the exertions necessary for preserving it; if they will not fight for it when it is directly attacked; if they can be deluded by the artifices used to cheat them out of it; if by momentary discouragement, or temporary panic, or a fit of enthusiasm for an individual, they can be induced to lay their liberties at the feet even of a great man, or trust him with powers which enable him to subvert their institutions; in all these cases they are more or less unfit for liberty: and . . . they are unlikely long to enjoy it. (John Stuart Mill)

The Cup of Elijah   כוס של אליהו

*The cups are re-filled. If desired, the Cup
of Elijah is passed around, with each
person pouring a little wine
into that cup.*

The door is opened

Leader:

Why do we drink four cups of wine at this service? Our tradition
is rich in answers:

Reader:

Each cup stands for the promise of freedom. We drink four cups to
say: let freedom reign in the four corners of the earth.

A Reader:

They are the four seasons. We drink the four cups to say: let
freedom reign in every season of the year.

A Reader:

They are the 'four empires' that oppressed us in days of old. We
drink the four cups to say: let tyranny pass away, let all the world
be free.

Leader:

And we drink the four cups in remembrance of the four divine
promises of redemption. As it is said: Say then to the people of
Israel:

All:

I am Adonai, and I will BRING YOU OUT from under the
Egyptian yoke.

I will DELIVER YOU from their bondage,

I will REDEEM YOU with outstretched arm.

I will TAKE YOU to be My people. . . .

71

But there is a *fifth* promise: ". . . and I will BRING YOU INTO the land. . . ." Should there then be a Fifth Cup? That question, says tradition, will not be answered until Elijah comes to proclaim the Messianic Time. Meanwhile it is a promise we remember with a cup from which we cannot drink, until all the world is redeemed from pain, injustice, denial of love. When will that time come?

A Reader:

The world is far from redemption. Our story, we have said, begins with degradation and ends with glory. Pain, injustice, denial of love: since our beginning we have known many degradations.

A Reader:

In every generation there are   בְּכָל־דּוֹר וָדוֹר

those who seek to destroy us . . .   . . . עוֹמְדִים עָלֵינוּ לְכַלּוֹתֵנוּ

All:

וְהַקָּדוֹשׁ בָּרוּךְ הוּא   V'hakadosh baruch hu
מַצִּילֵנוּ מִיָּדָם.   matsileinu miyadam.

But the Holy One saves us from their hands.

A Reader:

We remember expulsions and ghettos and inquisition.

A Reader:

We remember forced conversions and pogroms, enslavement and exile.

A Reader:

We remember the camps, a nightmare planet where one third of our people were reduced to ash.

All:

They have devoured Jacob	כִּי אָכַל אֶת־יַעֲקֹב
and laid waste our dwelling-places.	וְאֶת־נָוֵהוּ הֵשַׁמּוּ.

Leader:

But we have saved the Holy One	וְהַקָּדוֹשׁ בָּרוּךְ הוּא
from their hands!	הִצַּלְנוּ מִיָּדָם!

A Reader:

For from these fugitives, these oppressed, these martyrs came deeds of justice, and love, and truth. They are the people of Torah, children of the prophets; their forebears wrote Psalms of Praise.

All:

We shall remember. We shall not forget.
Praised is the one who remembers the glory!
Praised is the one who lingers over the telling!

73

Leader:

We remember many glories: we have married and raised children. We have sung God's praises. We have worked and rested, loved and laughed. The very land for which we braved the wilderness, in which we made our home: to that same land our people have returned, to build and be rebuilt.

All:

Zion heard and was glad;
the daughters of Judah rejoiced.

שָׁמְעָה וַתִּשְׂמַח צִיּוֹן;
וַתָּגֵלְנָה בְּנוֹת יְהוּדָה.

Leader:

But the full glory is still far from sight. Ignorance, prejudice, hatred; contempt for truth and justice; hunger and terror; the fear of a world-destroying war—these remain to plague the human race. To end these plagues, to summon Elijah—that is the task of all who care. It is *our* task, for we are the people who know the

stranger's heart, the slave's aching bones, the shaking hands of the exile. When will Elijah come with the news of freedom? When we have called him by our deeds. Then we shall say:

All:

I will lift up the cup of salvation, and call upon the name of God.

כּוֹס יְשׁוּעוֹת אֶשָּׂא,
וּבְשֵׁם יְיָ אֶקְרָא.

Leader:

Again, and yet again, we look into the future with a question on our lips and in our hearts. When shall we find answers that do not puzzle us? Where shall we find a drink that does not make us thirst all the more for having swallowed it?

A Reader:

Tonight we have asked questions and recited answers, although we know that every answer becomes a new question. For we know too that each new question may lead us to another answer.

Leader:

In the lore of our people one figure stands for all who have these two gifts: the gift of asking a question, the gift of listening to an answer.

A Reader:

Elijah, who challenged power with the question of justice.
I Kings 21

A Reader:

Elijah, whose own question to God found its answer in a still, small voice whispering within him.　　　　I Kings 19

A Reader:

Elijah, herald of reconciliation in time to come, when questions and answers shall flow among us. In our love, we shall come to understand. Then our redemption shall begin. As it is written:

75

הִנֵּה אָנֹכִי שֹׁלֵחַ לָכֶם אֵלִיָּהוּ הַנָּבִיא לִפְנֵי בּוֹא יוֹם יְיָ הַגָּדוֹל
וְהַנּוֹרָא: וְהֵשִׁיב לֵב אָבוֹת עַל בָּנִים, וְלֵב בָּנִים עַל אֲבוֹתָם.

"Behold, I am sending to you Elijah the prophet before
the coming of the great and awesome day of the
Eternal One: to turn the hearts of parents to their
children, and the hearts of children to their parents."

Leader:

And ON THAT DAY the promise of promises shall be fulfilled. As it is written:

All:

וְהֵבֵאתִי אֶתְכֶם אֶל V'HEIVEITI et-chem el
הָאָרֶץ. . . . ha-arets. . . .

And I will BRING YOU INTO the land. . . .   Exodus 6.8

Leader:

Israel and all the world shall reach the Land of Promise.

All:

בִּמְהֵרָה בְיָמֵינוּ. אָמֵן.

SPEEDILY, IN OUR DAYS. AMEN.

The door is closed

All:

♪

p. 103

אֵלִיָּהוּ הַנָּבִיא, אֵלִיָּהוּ   Ei-li-ya-hu ha-na-vi, Ei-li-ya-hu
הַתִּשְׁבִּי; אֵלִיָּהוּ, אֵלִיָּהוּ,   ha-tish-bi; Ei-li-ya-hu, Ei-li-ya-hu,
אֵלִיָּהוּ הַגִּלְעָדִי.   Ei-li-ya-hu ha-gil-a-di.
בִּמְהֵרָה בְיָמֵינוּ, יָבֹא   Bim-hei-ra v'ya-mei-nu, ya-vo
אֵלֵינוּ; עִם מָשִׁיחַ בֶּן   ei-lei-nu; im ma-shi-ach ben
דָּוִד, עִם מָשִׁיחַ בֶּן   Da-vid, im ma-shi-ach ben
דָּוִד. אֵלִיָּהוּ. . . .   Da-vid. Ei-li-ya-hu. . . .

*   *

77

"TODAY"

Rabbi Yehoshua once came upon the prophet Elijah
at the entrance of the cave
of Rabbi Shimon bar Yochai.
Yehoshua asked:
When will the Messiah come?
Go ask him, said the prophet.
He sits at the gates of Rome,
like all the poor.
His body is covered with running sores,
as is theirs.
This is how you can tell him apart from them:
When they want to apply fresh bandages,
the others first remove all the old dressings.
Not so with him—
he never changes more than one dressing at a time,
for he thinks:
I must be ready to answer the call without delay!
Rabbi Yehoshua went to Rome's gates and found him.
He said: Shalom to you, Master and Teacher!
The reply was: Shalom to you, Son of Levi!
Yehoshua then asked: Master, when are you coming?
And the answer was: Today!
Yehoshua left with a full heart,
and returned to his place.
But the day passed,
and with the fall of eve
no change could be seen.
Yehoshua turned to Elijah and wept:
The Messiah lied! Today! he said, yet he did not come . . .
But Elijah said: You must understand what he meant.
Is is not written?
"Today—if you will but listen to God's voice." (Psalm 95.7)
(Talmud)

Conclusion

נרצה

Leader:

Our celebration must not end before we remember our duty to remember. As it is said:

"As you rejoice before Adonai your God—you, your son and daughter, the stranger, the orphan, and the widow in your midst—

וְשָׂמַחְתָּ לִפְנֵי
יְיָ אֱלֹהֶיךָ – אַתָּה
וּבִנְךָ וּבִתֶּךָ, וְהַגֵּר
וְהַיָּתוֹם וְהָאַלְמָנָה
אֲשֶׁר בְּקִרְבֶּךָ –

All:

"Remember that you were a slave in the land of Egypt."

וְזָכַרְתָּ כִּי־עֶבֶד הָיִיתָ
בְּמִצְרָיִם.

Leader:

May our remembering lead to acts of love and kindness, for we know the ache in the stranger's heart:

All:

"The strangers in your midst shall be to you as the native-born, and you shall love them as yourselves, for you were strangers in the land of Egypt."

כְּאֶזְרָח מִכֶּם יִהְיֶה לָכֶם
הַגֵּר הַגָּר אִתְּכֶם,
וְאָהַבְתָּ לוֹ כָּמוֹךָ,
כִּי גֵרִים הֱיִיתֶם בְּאֶרֶץ
מִצְרָיִם.

Leader:

There shall be among us neither master nor slave, as it is said:

All:

"Only Me shall the people of Israel serve; they are My servants whom I brought out of the land of Egypt; I am Adonai your God."

כִּי־לִי בְנֵי יִשְׂרָאֵל
עֲבָדִים; עֲבָדַי הֵם
אֲשֶׁר הוֹצֵאתִי אוֹתָם
מֵאֶרֶץ מִצְרָיִם.
אֲנִי יְיָ אֱלֹהֵיכֶם.

*   *

Leader:

Our redemption is not yet complete, but as we raise the final cup of wine in remembrance of the fourth promise of redemption, our hearts beat strong with hope. For it is said:

All:

וְלָקַחְתִּי אֶתְכֶם לִי לְעָם,   V'LAKACHTI et-chem li l'am,
וְהָיִיתִי לָכֶם לֵאלֹהִים.   v'hayiti lachem leilohim.

I will TAKE YOU to be My people, and I will be your God.

בָּרוּךְ אַתָּה יְיָ, אֱלֹהֵינוּ
מֶלֶךְ הָעוֹלָם, בּוֹרֵא פְּרִי
הַגָּפֶן.

Baruch ata Adonai, Eloheinu
melech ha-olam, borei p'ri
hagafen.

We praise You, Eternal God, Ruler of time and space,
Creator of the fruit of the vine.

בָּרוּךְ אַתָּה יְיָ, אֱלֹהֵינוּ
מֶלֶךְ הָעוֹלָם, שֶׁעָשָׂנוּ
בְּנֵי חוֹרִין.

Baruch ata Adonai, Eloheinu
melech ha-olam, she-asanu
b'nei chorin.

We praise You, Eternal God, Ruler of time and space,
who has made us to be free.

All now drink the fourth cup

*   *

Leader:

חֲסַל סִדּוּר פֶּסַח כְּהִלְכָתוֹ,
כְּכָל־מִשְׁפָּטוֹ וְחֻקָּתוֹ.
כַּאֲשֶׁר זָכִינוּ לְסַדֵּר אוֹתוֹ,
כֵּן נִזְכֶּה לַעֲשׂוֹתוֹ.

Our Seder now concludes,
its rites and customs done.
This year's task completed,
we look to a time yet unborn.
We look to the light of dawn,
tomorrow's promised Passover,
the days of peace, the days of love,
the time of full redemption.

All:

Tomorrow's promised Passover:
the days of peace,
the days of love,
the time of full redemption.

Leader:

וְיָשְׁבוּ אִישׁ תַּחַת גַּפְנוֹ וְתַחַת תְּאֵנָתוֹ, וְאֵין מַחֲרִיד.

Then all shall sit under their vines and under their fig-
trees, and none shall make them afraid.

All:

FOR US AND ALL ISRAEL,	לָנוּ וּלְכָל-בֵּית יִשְׂרָאֵל,
FOR US AND ALL HUMANKIND:	לָנוּ וּלְכָל-יוֹשְׁבֵי תֵבֵל:
NEXT YEAR IN JERUSALEM!	לַשָּׁנָה הַבָּאָה בִּירוּשָׁלָיִם!
NEXT YEAR	לַשָּׁנָה הַבָּאָה
ALL THE WORLD REDEEMED!	כָּל-חַי נִגְאָל!

*   *

פרקי שירה

כי לו נאה

Transliteration, p. 84; translation, p. 85

כִּי לוֹ נָאֶה. כִּי לוֹ יָאֶה.

אַדִּיר בִּמְלוּכָה, בָּחוּר כַּהֲלָכָה, גְּדוּדָיו יֹאמְרוּ לוֹ:
לְךָ וּלְךָ, לְךָ כִּי לְךָ, לְךָ אַף לְךָ, לְךָ יְיָ הַמַּמְלָכָה.
כִּי לוֹ נָאֶה, כִּי לוֹ יָאֶה.

דָּגוּל בִּמְלוּכָה, הָדוּר כַּהֲלָכָה, וָתִיקָיו יֹאמְרוּ לוֹ:
לְךָ וּלְךָ, לְךָ כִּי לְךָ, לְךָ אַף לְךָ, לְךָ יְיָ הַמַּמְלָכָה.
כִּי לוֹ נָאֶה, כִּי לוֹ יָאֶה.

זַכַּאי בִּמְלוּכָה, חָסִין כַּהֲלָכָה, טַפְסְרָיו יֹאמְרוּ לוֹ:
לְךָ וּלְךָ, לְךָ כִּי לְךָ, לְךָ אַף לְךָ, לְךָ יְיָ הַמַּמְלָכָה.
כִּי לוֹ נָאֶה, כִּי לוֹ יָאֶה.

יָחִיד בִּמְלוּכָה, כַּבִּיר כַּהֲלָכָה, לִמּוּדָיו יֹאמְרוּ לוֹ:
לְךָ וּלְךָ, לְךָ כִּי לְךָ, לְךָ אַף לְךָ, לְךָ יְיָ הַמַּמְלָכָה.
כִּי לוֹ נָאֶה, כִּי לוֹ יָאֶה.

מָרוֹם בִּמְלוּכָה, נוֹרָא כַּהֲלָכָה, סְבִיבָיו יֹאמְרוּ לוֹ:
לְךָ וּלְךָ, לְךָ כִּי לְךָ, לְךָ אַף לְךָ, לְךָ יְיָ הַמַּמְלָכָה.
כִּי לוֹ נָאֶה, כִּי לוֹ יָאֶה.

עָנָיו בִּמְלוּכָה, פּוֹדֶה כַּהֲלָכָה, צַדִּיקָיו יֹאמְרוּ לוֹ:
לְךָ וּלְךָ, לְךָ כִּי לְךָ, לְךָ אַף לְךָ, לְךָ יְיָ הַמַּמְלָכָה.
כִּי לוֹ נָאֶה, כִּי לוֹ יָאֶה.

קָדוֹשׁ בִּמְלוּכָה, רַחוּם כַּהֲלָכָה, שִׁנְאַנָּיו יֹאמְרוּ לוֹ:
לְךָ וּלְךָ, לְךָ כִּי לְךָ, לְךָ אַף לְךָ, לְךָ יְיָ הַמַּמְלָכָה.
כִּי לוֹ נָאֶה, כִּי לוֹ יָאֶה.

תַּקִּיף בִּמְלוּכָה, תּוֹמֵךְ כַּהֲלָכָה, תְּמִימָיו יֹאמְרוּ לוֹ:
לְךָ וּלְךָ, לְךָ כִּי לְךָ, לְךָ אַף לְךָ, לְךָ יְיָ הַמַּמְלָכָה.
כִּי לוֹ נָאֶה, כִּי לוֹ יָאֶה.

Ki lo na-eh, ki lo ya-eh.

Adir bim-lucha, Bachur ka-halacha,
Gedudav yom'ru lo:
l'cha u-l'cha, l'cha ki l'cha, l'cha af l'cha, l'cha Adonai ha-mamlacha.
Ki lo na-eh, ki lo ya-eh.

Dagul bim-lucha, Hadur ka-halacha,
Vatikav yom'ru lo:
l'cha u-l'cha, l'cha ki l'cha, l'cha af l'cha, l'cha Adonai ha-mamlacha.
Ki lo na-eh, ki lo ya-eh.

Zakai bim-lucha, CHasin ka-halacha,
Taf-s'rav yom'ru lo:
l'cha u-l'cha, l'cha ki l'cha, l'ch af l'cha, l'cha Adonai ha-mamlacha.
Ki lo na-eh, ki lo ya-eh.

Yachid bim-lucha, Kabir ka-halacha,
Limudav yom'ru lo:
l'cha u-l'cha, l'cha ki l'cha, l'cha af l'cha, l'cha Adonai ha-mamlacha.
Ki lo na-eh, ki lo ya-eh.

Marom bim-lucha, Nora ka-halacha,
S'vivav yom'ru lo:
l'cha u-l'cha, l'cha ki l'cha, l'cha af l'cha, l'cha Adonai ha-mamlacha.
Ki lo na-eh, ki lo ya-eh.

Anav bim-lucha, Podeh ka-halacha,
TSadikav yom'ru lo:
l'cha u-l'cha, l'cha ki l'cha, l'cha af l'cha, l'cha Adonai ha-mamlacha.
Ki lo na-eh, ki lo ya-eh.

Kadosh bim-lucha, Rachum ka-halacha,
SHin-anav yom'ru lo:
l'cha u-l'cha, l'cha ki l'cha, l'cha af l'cha, l'cha Adonai ha-mamlacha.
Ki lo na-eh, ki lo ya-eh.

Takif bim-lucha, Tomeich ka-halacha,
T'mimav yom'ru lo:
l'cha u-l'cha, l'cha ki l'cha, l'cha af l'cha, l'cha Adonai ha-mamlacha.
Ki lo na-eh, ki lo ya-eh.

*   *

To You praise belongs;
to You praise is due.

Almighty in rule,
Beloved by right,
Your Chosen ones sing:
Yours only, Yours solely, Yours alone, God, is the dominion.
To You praise belongs,
to You praise is due.

Dominant in rule,
Excelling by right,
Your Faithful ones sing:
Yours only. . . .

Glorious in rule,
Hallowed by right,
Your just ones sing:
Yours only. . . .

Kindly in rule,
Lawgiver by right,
Your Ministers sing:
Yours only. . . .

Nonpareil in rule,
Omnipresent by right,
Your People sing:
Yours only. . . .

Resplendent in Rule,
Sovereign by right,
Your Thankful ones sing:
Yours only. . . .

Unrivalled in rule,
Your Worshippers sing:
Yours only. . . .

Worthy of rule,
Wonderful by right,
Your Witnesses sing:
Yours only. . . .

*   *

אַדִּיר הוּא, יִגְאָלֵנוּ בְּקָרוֹב,
בִּמְהֵרָה בִּמְהֵרָה בְּיָמֵינוּ בְּקָרוֹב.
אֵל פְּדֵה, אֵל פְּדֵה, פְּדֵה עַמְּךָ בְּקָרוֹב.

♪

p. 103

בָּחוּר הוּא, גָּדוֹל הוּא, דָּגוּל הוּא,
יִגְאָלֵנוּ בְּקָרוֹב, בִּמְהֵרָה בִּמְהֵרָה בְּיָמֵינוּ
בְּקָרוֹב. אֵל פְּדֵה, אֵל פְּדֵה, פְּדֵה עַמְּךָ בְּקָרוֹב.

הָדוּר הוּא, וָתִיק הוּא, זַכַּאי הוּא,
יִגְאָלֵנוּ בְּקָרוֹב, בִּמְהֵרָה בִּמְהֵרָה בְּיָמֵינוּ
בְּקָרוֹב. אֵל פְּדֵה, אֵל פְּדֵה, פְּדֵה עַמְּךָ בְּקָרוֹב.

חָסִיד הוּא, טָהוֹר הוּא, יָחִיד הוּא,
יִגְאָלֵנוּ בְּקָרוֹב, בִּמְהֵרָה בִּמְהֵרָה בְּיָמֵינוּ
בְּקָרוֹב. אֵל פְּדֵה, אֵל פְּדֵה, פְּדֵה עַמְּךָ בְּקָרוֹב.

כַּבִּיר הוּא, לָמוּד הוּא, מֶלֶךְ הוּא,
יִגְאָלֵנוּ בְּקָרוֹב, בִּמְהֵרָה בִּמְהֵרָה בְּיָמֵינוּ
בְּקָרוֹב. אֵל פְּדֵה, אֵל פְּדֵה, פְּדֵה עַמְּךָ בְּקָרוֹב.

נוֹרָא הוּא, סַגִּיב הוּא, עִזּוּז הוּא,
יִגְאָלֵנוּ בְּקָרוֹב, בִּמְהֵרָה בִּמְהֵרָה בְּיָמֵינוּ
בְּקָרוֹב. אֵל פְּדֵה, אֵל פְּדֵה, פְּדֵה עַמְּךָ בְּקָרוֹב.

פּוֹדֶה הוּא, צַדִּיק הוּא, קָדוֹשׁ הוּא,
יִגְאָלֵנוּ בְּקָרוֹב, בִּמְהֵרָה בִּמְהֵרָה בְּיָמֵינוּ
בְּקָרוֹב. אֵל פְּדֵה, אֵל פְּדֵה, פְּדֵה עַמְּךָ בְּקָרוֹב.

רַחוּם הוּא, שַׁדַּי הוּא, תַּקִּיף הוּא,
יִגְאָלֵנוּ בְּקָרוֹב, בִּמְהֵרָה בִּמְהֵרָה בְּיָמֵינוּ
בְּקָרוֹב. אֵל פְּדֵה, אֵל פְּדֵה, פְּדֵה עַמְּךָ בְּקָרוֹב.

Adir hu (2), yig-aleinu b'karov,
bim-heira, bim-heira
b'yameinu b'karov
El p'dei, El p'dei, p'dei am'cha b'karov.

Bachur hu, gadol hu, Dagul hu,
yig-aleinu b'karov, bim-heira bim-heira
b'yameinu b'karov.
El p'dei, El p'dei, p'dei am'cha b'karov.

CHasid hu, Tahor hu, Yachid hu,
yig-aleinu b'karov, bim-heira bim-heira
b'yameinu b'karov.
El p'dei, El p'dei, p'dei am'cha b'karov.

Kabir hu, Lamud hu, Melech hu,
yig-aleinu b'karov, bim-heira bim-heira
b'yameinu b'karov.
El p'dei, El p'dei, p'dei am'cha b'karov.

Nora hu, Sagiv hu, Izuz hu,
yig-aleinu b'karov, bim-heira bim-heira
b'yameinu b'karov.
El p'dei, El p'dei, p'dei am'cha b'karov.

Podeh hu, TSadik hu, Kadosh hu,
yig-aleinu b'karov, bim-heira bim-heira
b'yameinu b'karov.
El p'dei, El p'dei, p'dei am'cha b'karov.

Rachum hu, SHaddai hu, Takif hu,
yig-aleinu b'karov, bim-heira bim-heira
b'yameinu b'karov.
El p'dei, El p'dei, p'dei am'cha b'karov.

*   *

Awesome One (2), soon may You redeem us,
speedily, speedily,
soon within our lifetime.
Save, O God; save, O God,
save Your people speedily.

Blessed One, Caring One, Devoted One,
soon may You redeem us,
etc.

Endless One, Faithful One, Gracious One,
soon may You redeem us,
etc.

Holy One, Infinite One, Joying One,
soon may You redeem us,
etc.

Knowing One, Loving One, Mighty One,
soon may You redeem us,
etc.

Noble One, Only One, Perfect One,
soon may You redeem us,
etc.

Righteous One, Saving One, Teaching One
soon may You redeem us,
etc.

Unique One, Valiant One, Wisest One,
soon may You redeem us,
etc.

*   *

GOD OF MIGHT

God of might, God of right,
Rock of our salvation,
Unto You still we do
Offer adoration,
Since Your hand from Egypt's land
Led Your joyful nation.

God of all, when we call,
On Your love unending,
Save and hear; O be near,
Unto us extending
Power benign, grace divine
In our hearts descending.

Mighty God, by Your rod
Freedom first was given.
Now as then, let again
Bonds and chains be riven,
You our trust, wise and just,
God of earth and heaven.

*   *

אֶחָד מִי יוֹדֵעַ, אֶחָד אֲנִי יוֹדֵעַ: אֶחָד אֱלֹהֵינוּ שֶׁבַּשָּׁמַיִם וּבָאָרֶץ.

♪
p. 104

שְׁנַיִם מִי יוֹדֵעַ, שְׁנַיִם אֲנִי יוֹדֵעַ: שְׁנֵי לֻחוֹת הַבְּרִית, אֶחָד אֱלֹהֵינוּ שֶׁבַּשָּׁמַיִם וּבָאָרֶץ.

שְׁלֹשָׁה מִי יוֹדֵעַ, שְׁלֹשָׁה אֲנִי יוֹדֵעַ: שְׁלֹשָׁה אָבוֹת, שְׁנֵי לֻחוֹת הַבְּרִית, אֶחָד אֱלֹהֵינוּ שֶׁבַּשָּׁמַיִם וּבָאָרֶץ.

אַרְבַּע מִי יוֹדֵעַ, אַרְבַּע אֲנִי יוֹדֵעַ: אַרְבַּע אִמָּהוֹת, שְׁלֹשָׁה אָבוֹת, שְׁנֵי לֻחוֹת הַבְּרִית, אֶחָד אֱלֹהֵינוּ שֶׁבַּשָּׁמַיִם וּבָאָרֶץ.

חֲמִשָּׁה מִי יוֹדֵעַ, חֲמִשָּׁה אֲנִי יוֹדֵעַ: חֲמִשָּׁה חֻמְשֵׁי תוֹרָה, אַרְבַּע אִמָּהוֹת, שְׁלֹשָׁה אָבוֹת, שְׁנֵי לֻחוֹת הַבְּרִית, אֶחָד אֱלֹהֵינוּ שֶׁבַּשָּׁמַיִם וּבָאָרֶץ.

שִׁשָּׁה מִי יוֹדֵעַ, שִׁשָּׁה אֲנִי יוֹדֵעַ: שִׁשָּׁה סִדְרֵי מִשְׁנָה, חֲמִשָּׁה חֻמְשֵׁי תוֹרָה, אַרְבַּע אִמָּהוֹת, שְׁלֹשָׁה אָבוֹת, שְׁנֵי לֻחוֹת הַבְּרִית, אֶחָד אֱלֹהֵינוּ שֶׁבַּשָּׁמַיִם וּבָאָרֶץ.

שִׁבְעָה מִי יוֹדֵעַ, שִׁבְעָה אֲנִי יוֹדֵעַ: שִׁבְעָה יְמֵי שַׁבַּתָּא, שִׁשָּׁה סִדְרֵי מִשְׁנָה, חֲמִשָּׁה חֻמְשֵׁי תוֹרָה, אַרְבַּע אִמָּהוֹת, שְׁלֹשָׁה אָבוֹת, שְׁנֵי לֻחוֹת הַבְּרִית, אֶחָד אֱלֹהֵינוּ שֶׁבַּשָּׁמַיִם וּבָאָרֶץ.

שְׁמוֹנָה מִי יוֹדֵעַ, שְׁמוֹנָה אֲנִי יוֹדֵעַ: שְׁמוֹנָה יְמֵי מִילָה, שִׁבְעָה יְמֵי שַׁבַּתָּא, שִׁשָּׁה סִדְרֵי מִשְׁנָה, חֲמִשָּׁה חֻמְשֵׁי תוֹרָה, אַרְבַּע אִמָּהוֹת, שְׁלֹשָׁה אָבוֹת, שְׁנֵי לֻחוֹת הַבְּרִית, אֶחָד אֱלֹהֵינוּ שֶׁבַּשָּׁמַיִם וּבָאָרֶץ.

תִּשְׁעָה מִי יוֹדֵעַ, תִּשְׁעָה אֲנִי יוֹדֵעַ: תִּשְׁעָה יַרְחֵי לֵדָה, שְׁמוֹנָה יְמֵי מִילָה, שִׁבְעָה יְמֵי שַׁבַּתָּא, שִׁשָּׁה סִדְרֵי מִשְׁנָה, חֲמִשָּׁה חֻמְשֵׁי תוֹרָה, אַרְבַּע אִמָּהוֹת, שְׁלֹשָׁה אָבוֹת, שְׁנֵי לֻחוֹת הַבְּרִית, אֶחָד אֱלֹהֵינוּ שֶׁבַּשָּׁמַיִם וּבָאָרֶץ.

עֲשָׂרָה מִי יוֹדֵעַ, עֲשָׂרָה אֲנִי יוֹדֵעַ: עֲשָׂרָה דִבְּרַיָּא, תִּשְׁעָה יַרְחֵי לֵדָה, שְׁמוֹנָה יְמֵי מִילָה, שִׁבְעָה יְמֵי שַׁבַּתָּא, שִׁשָּׁה סִדְרֵי מִשְׁנָה, חֲמִשָּׁה חֻמְשֵׁי תוֹרָה, אַרְבַּע אִמָּהוֹת, שְׁלֹשָׁה אָבוֹת, שְׁנֵי לֻחוֹת הַבְּרִית, אֶחָד אֱלֹהֵינוּ שֶׁבַּשָּׁמַיִם וּבָאָרֶץ.

אַחַד עָשָׂר מִי יוֹדֵעַ, אַחַד עָשָׂר אֲנִי יוֹדֵעַ: אַחַד עָשָׂר
כּוֹכְבַיָּא, עֲשָׂרָה דִבְּרַיָּא, תִּשְׁעָה יַרְחֵי לֵדָה, שְׁמוֹנָה יְמֵי
מִילָה, שִׁבְעָה יְמֵי שַׁבַּתָּא, שִׁשָּׁה סִדְרֵי מִשְׁנָה, חֲמִשָּׁה
חֻמְשֵׁי תוֹרָה, אַרְבַּע אִמָּהוֹת, שְׁלֹשָׁה אָבוֹת, שְׁנֵי לֻחוֹת
הַבְּרִית, אֶחָד אֱלֹהֵינוּ שֶׁבַּשָּׁמַיִם וּבָאָרֶץ.

שְׁנֵים עָשָׂר מִי יוֹדֵעַ, שְׁנֵים עָשָׂר אֲנִי יוֹדֵעַ: שְׁנֵים עָשָׂר
שִׁבְטַיָּא, אַחַד עָשָׂר כּוֹכְבַיָּא, עֲשָׂרָה דִבְּרַיָּא, תִּשְׁעָה יַרְחֵי
לֵדָה, שְׁמוֹנָה יְמֵי מִילָה, שִׁבְעָה יְמֵי שַׁבַּתָּא, שִׁשָּׁה סִדְרֵי
מִשְׁנָה, חֲמִשָּׁה חֻמְשֵׁי תוֹרָה, אַרְבַּע אִמָּהוֹת, שְׁלֹשָׁה אָבוֹת,
שְׁנֵי לֻחוֹת הַבְּרִית, אֶחָד אֱלֹהֵינוּ שֶׁבַּשָּׁמַיִם וּבָאָרֶץ.

שְׁלֹשָׁה עָשָׂר מִי יוֹדֵעַ, שְׁלֹשָׁה עָשָׂר אֲנִי יוֹדֵעַ: שְׁלֹשָׁה עָשָׂר
מִדַּיָּא, שְׁנֵים עָשָׂר שִׁבְטַיָּא, אַחַד עָשָׂר כּוֹכְבַיָּא, עֲשָׂרָה
דִבְּרַיָּא, תִּשְׁעָה יַרְחֵי לֵדָה, שְׁמוֹנָה יְמֵי מִילָה, שִׁבְעָה יְמֵי
שַׁבַּתָּא, שִׁשָּׁה סִדְרֵי מִשְׁנָה, חֲמִשָּׁה חֻמְשֵׁי תוֹרָה, אַרְבַּע
אִמָּהוֹת, שְׁלֹשָׁה אָבוֹת, שְׁנֵי לֻחוֹת הַבְּרִית, אֶחָד אֱלֹהֵינוּ
שֶׁבַּשָּׁמַיִם וּבָאָרֶץ.

*　　　　　*

Who knows One? I know One.
One is almighty God, almighty God, almighty God, almighty God,
who reigns in heaven and upon the earth,
who reigns in heaven and upon the earth.

♪

p. 104

Who knows two? I know two.
Two tables of the Law, One is almighty God,
almighty God, almighty God, almighty God,
who reigns in heaven and upon the earth,
who reigns in heaven and upon the earth.

Who knows three? I know three.
Three is the Patriarchs, Two tables of the Law, One is almighty
God, almighty God, almighty God, almighty God, who reigns in
heaven. . . .

Who knows four? I know four.
Four is the Matriarchs, Three is the Patriarchs, Two tables of the
Law, One is almighty God, almighty God. . . .

Who knows five? I know five.
Five books of Moses, Four is the Matriarchs, Three is the
Patriarchs, Two tables of the Law, One is almighty God, almighty
God. . . .

Who knows six? I know six. Six are the Mishnah's Orders, Five
books of Moses, Four is the Matriarchs, Three is the Patriarchs,
Two tables of the Law, One is almighty God, almighty God. . . .

Who knows seven? I know seven.
Seven days make up a week, Six are the Mishnah's Orders, Five
books of Moses, Four is the Matriarchs, Three is the Patriarchs,
Two tables of the Law, One is almighty God. . . .

Who knows eight? I know eight.
Eight days are for a B'rit, Seven days make up a week, Six are the
Mishnah's Orders, Five books of Moses, Four is the Matriarchs,
Three is the Patriarchs, Two tables of the Law, One is almighty
God, almighty God. . . .

91

Who knows nine? I know nine.

Nine months to childbirth, Eight days are for a B'rit, Seven days make up a week, Six are the Mishnah's Orders, Five books of Moses, Four is the Matriarchs, Three is the Patriarchs, Two tables of the Law, One is almighty God, almighty God. . . .

Who knows ten? I know ten.

Ten for the Commandments, Nine months to childbirth, Eight days are for a B'rit, Seven days make up a week, Six are the Mishnah's Orders, Five books of Moses, Four is the Matriarchs, Three is the Patriarchs, Two tables of the Law, One is almighty God, almighty God. . . .

Who knows eleven? I know eleven.

Eleven stars in Joseph's dream, Ten for the Commandments, Nine months to childbirth, Eight days are for a B'rit, Seven days make up a week, Six are the Mishnah's orders, Five books of Moses, Four is the Matriarchs, Three is the Patriarchs, Two tables of the Law, One is almighty God, almighty God. . . .

Who knows twelve? I know twelve.

Twelve tribes of Israel, Eleven Stars in Joseph's dream, Ten for the Commandments, Nine months to childbirth, Eight days are for a B'rit, Seven days make up a week, Six are the Mishnah's Orders, Five books of Moses, Four is the Matriarchs, Three is the Patriarchs, Two tables of the Law, One is almighty God, almighty God. . . .

Who knows thirteen? I know thirteen.

Thirteen Attributes of God, Twelve tribes of Israel, Eleven stars in Joseph's dream, Ten for the Commandments, Nine months to childbirth, Eight days are for a B'rit, Seven days make up a week, Six are the Mishnah's Orders, Five books of Moses, Four is the Matriarchs, Three is the Patriarchs, Two tables of the Law, One is almighty God, almighty God. . . .

*   *

KAREIV YOM קרב יום

p. 104

קָרֵב יוֹם אֲשֶׁר הוּא לֹא יוֹם
וְלֹא לַיְלָה.
רָם הוֹדַע כִּי לְךָ הַיּוֹם
אַף לְךָ הַלַּיְלָה.
שׁוֹמְרִים הַפְקֵד לְעִירְךָ
כָּל־הַיּוֹם וְכָל־הַלַּיְלָה.
תָּאִיר כְּאוֹר יוֹם חֶשְׁכַת לַיְלָה.

Kareiv yom asher hu lo yom
v'lo laila.
Ram hoda ki l'cha hayom
af l'cha halaila.
Shom'rim hafkeid l'ir'cha
kol hayom v'chol halaila
Ta-ir k'or yom chesh-chat laila.

Bring near the day that is neither day nor night.
Declare, Most High, that the day is Yours, and Yours the night.
Place sentries over Your City all the day and all the night.
Make bright as the light of day the darkness of night.

*   *

ANA HALACH DODEICH אנה הלך דודך

p. 105

אָנָה הָלַךְ דּוֹדֵךְ,
הַיָּפָה בַּנָּשִׁים?
אָנָה פָּנָה דוֹדֵךְ?
וּנְבַקְשֶׁנּוּ עִמָּךְ.
דּוֹדִי יָרַד לְגַנּוֹ, לַעֲרוּגוֹת הַבְּשֶׂם.

Ana halach dodeich,
ha-yafa ba-nashim?
Ana pana dodeich?
U-n'vakshenu imach.
Dodi yarad l'gano, la-arugot ha-bosem.

Where has your love gone, O fairest of women?
Where has your love gone to? Let us help you seek him.
My love has gone to his garden, to the beds of spices.

*   *

DODI LI דודי לי

דּוֹדִי לִי וַאֲנִי לוֹ,
הָרֹעֶה בַּשּׁוֹשַׁנִּים.
מִי זֹאת עֹלָה מִן הַמִּדְבָּר,
מִי זֹאת עֹלָה?
מְקֻטֶּרֶת מוֹר, מוֹר וּלְבוֹנָה,
מוֹר וּלְבוֹנָה.
לִבַּבְתִּנִי, אֲחֹתִי כַלָּה,
לִבַּבְתִּנִי כַלָּה.
עוּרִי צָפוֹן, וּבוֹאִי תֵימָן,
עוּרִי צָפוֹן, וּבוֹאִי תֵימָן.

Dodi li va-ani lo,
ha-ro-eh ba-shoshanim.
Mi zot olah min ha-midbar,
mi zot olah?
M'kuteret mor, mor u-l'vona,
mor u-l'vonah.
Libavtini, achoti kala,
libavtini kalah.
Uri tsafon, u-vo-i teiman,
uri tsafon, u-vo-i teiman.

93

My beloved is mine, and I am his, who pastures among the lilies.
Who is that coming out of the desert, who is it?
Anointed with myrrh, myrrh and frankincense. . . .
You have taken my heart, my sister, my bride; you have taken my heart.
Rise up, O North Wind, and come, O South wind.

*   *

EL GINAT EGOZ   אל גנת אגוז

אֵל גַּנַת אֱגוֹז יָרַדְתִּי	El ginat egoz yarad'ti
לִרְאוֹת בְּאִבֵּי הַנָּחַל,	lir-ot b'ibei ha-nachal,
לִרְאוֹת הֲפָרְחָה הַגֶּפֶן,	lir-ot ha-far'cha ha-gefen,
הֵנֵצוּ הָרִמוֹנִים.	heineitsu ha-rimonim.
לְכָה דוֹדִי, נֵצֵא הַשָּׂדֶה,	L'cha dodi, neitsei ha-sadeh,
נָלִינָה בַּכְּפָרִים, נַשְׁכִּימָה לַכְּרָמִים	nalina ba-k'farim, nashkima la-k'ramim
נִרְאֶה אִם פָּרְחָה הַגֶּפֶן	nir-eh im par'cha ha-gefen
פִּתַּח הַסְּמָדַר.	pitach ha-s'madar.
עוּרִי צָפוֹן וּבוֹאִי תֵימָן	U-ri tsafon u-vo-i teiman
הָפִיחִי גַנִּי, יִזְּלוּ בְשָׂמָיו	hafichi gani, yizlu v'samav
יָבֹא דוֹדִי לְגַנּוֹ	yavo dodi l'gano
וְיֹאכַל פְּרִי מְגָדָיו.	v'yochal p'ri m'gadav.

I went down to the grove to see the valley break into the flower, to see if the vines had blossomed, if the pomegranates were in bloom. Come, my beloved, let us go into the field and lie down among the flowers. Let us go early to the vineyards; let us see if the vine has flowered, if its blossoms have opened. Awake, O north wind, come, O south wind! Blow upon my garden, that its perfume may spread. Let my beloved come to his garden and enjoy its luscious fruits!

*   *

LET MY PEOPLE GO

When Israel was in Egypt land,
Let my people go.
Oppressed so hard they could not stand.
Let my people go.

Refrain
Go down Moses, way down in Egypt land,
Tell ol' Pharaoh, let my people go.

♪
p. 105
p. 106

Thus saith the Lord, bold Moses said,
Let my people go.

If not I'll smite your firstborn dead,
Let my people go.   (REFRAIN)

As Israel stood by the water side,
Let my people go.

By God's command it did divide,
Let my people go.   (REFRAIN)

*   *

חד גדיא   AN ONLY KID

♪

p. 106

חַד גַּדְיָא, חַד גַּדְיָא,
דְּזְבַן אַבָּא בִּתְרֵי זוּזֵי;
חַד גַּדְיָא, חַד גַּדְיָא.

Chad gadya, chad gadya,
diz'van aba bitrei zuzei;
chad gadya, chad gadya.

וְאָתָא שׁוּנְרָא וְאָכַל לְגַדְיָא,
דְּזְבַן אַבָּא בִּתְרֵי זוּזֵי;
חַד גַּדְיָא, חַד גַּדְיָא.

V'ata shunra v'achal l'gadya,
diz'van aba bitrei zuzei;
chad gadya, chad gadya.

וְאָתָא כַלְבָּא וְנָשַׁךְ לְשׁוּנְרָא,
דְּאָכַל לְגַדְיָא,
דְּזְבַן אַבָּא בִּתְרֵי זוּזֵי;
חַד גַּדְיָא, חַד גַּדְיָא.

V'ata chalba v'nashach l'shunra,
d'achal l'gadya,
diz'van aba bitrei zuzei;
chad gadya, chad gadya.

וְאָתָא חוּטְרָא וְהִכָּה לְכַלְבָּא,
דְּנָשַׁךְ לְשׁוּנְרָא, דְּאָכַל לְגַדְיָא,
דְּזְבַן אַבָּא בִּתְרֵי זוּזֵי;
חַד גַּדְיָא, חַד גַּדְיָא.

V'ata chutra v'hika l'chalba,
d'nashach l'shunra, d'achal l'gadya,
diz'van aba bitrei zuzei;
chad gadya, chad gadya.

וְאָתָא נוּרָא וְשָׂרַף לְחוּטְרָא,
דְּהִכָּה לְכַלְבָּא, דְּנָשַׁךְ לְשׁוּנְרָא,
דְּאָכַל לְגַדְיָא,
דְּזְבַן אַבָּא בִּתְרֵי זוּזֵי;
חַד גַּדְיָא, חַד גַּדְיָא.

V'ata nura v'saraf l'chutra,
d'hika l'chalba, d'nashach l'shunra,
d'achal l'gadya,
diz'van aba bitrei zuzei;
chad gadya, chad gadya.

95

וְאָתָא מַיָּא וְכָבָה לְנוּרָא,
דְּשָׂרַף לְחוּטְרָא, דְּהִכָּה לְכַלְבָּא,
דְּנָשַׁךְ לְשׁוּנְרָא, דְּאָכַל לְגַדְיָא,
דְּזַבֵּן אַבָּא בִּתְרֵי זוּזֵי;
חַד גַּדְיָא, חַד גַּדְיָא.

V'ata maya v'chava l'nura,
d'saraf l'chutra, d'hika l'chalba,
d'nashach l'shunra, d'achal l'gadya,
diz'van aba bitrei zuzei;
chad gadya, chad gadya.

וְאָתָא תוֹרָא וְשָׁתָא לְמַיָּא,
דְּכָבָה לְנוּרָא, דְּשָׂרַף לְחוּטְרָא,
דְּהִכָּה לְכַלְבָּא, דְּנָשַׁךְ לְשׁוּנְרָא,
דְּאָכַל לְגַדְיָא,
דְּזַבֵּן אַבָּא בִּתְרֵי זוּזֵי;
חַד גַּדְיָא, חַד גַּדְיָא.

V'ata tora v'shata l'maya,
d'chava l'nura, d'saraf l'chutra,
d'hika l'chalba, d'nashach l'shunra,
d'achal l'gadya,
diz'van aba bitrei zuzei;
chad gadya, chad gadya.

וְאָתָא הַשּׁוֹחֵט וְשָׁחַט לְתוֹרָא,
דְּשָׁתָה לְמַיָּא, דְּכָבָה לְנוּרָא,
דְּשָׂרַף לְחוּטְרָא, דְּהִכָּה לְכַלְבָּא,
דְּנָשַׁךְ לְשׁוּנְרָא, דְּאָכַל לְגַדְיָא,
דְּזַבֵּן אַבָּא בִּתְרֵי זוּזֵי;
חַד גַּדְיָא, חַד גַּדְיָא.

V'ata ha-shochet v'shachat l'tora,
d'shata l'maya, d'chava l'nura,
d'saraf l'chutra, d'hika l'chalba,
d'nashach l'shunra, d'achal l'gadya,
diz'van aba bitrei zuzei;
chad gadya, chad gadya.

וְאָתָא מַלְאַךְ הַמָּוֶת,
וְשָׁחַט לַשּׁוֹחֵט,
דְּשָׁחַט לְתוֹרָא, דְּשָׁתָה לְמַיָּא,
דְּכָבָה לְנוּרָא, דְּשָׂרַף לְחוּטְרָא,
דְּהִכָּה לְכַלְבָּא, דְּנָשַׁךְ לְשׁוּנְרָא,
דְּאָכַל לְגַדְיָא,
דְּזַבֵּן אַבָּא בִּתְרֵי זוּזֵי;
חַד גַּדְיָא, חַד גַּדְיָא.

V'ata mal-ach ha-mavet,
v'shachat la-shochet,
d'shachat l'tora, d'shata l'maya,
d'chava l'nura, d'saraf l'chutra,
d'hika l'chalba, d'nashach l'shunra,
d'achal l'gadya,
diz'van aba bitrei zuzei;
chad gadya, chad gadya.

וְאָתָא הַקָּדוֹשׁ בָּרוּךְ הוּא,
וְשָׁחַט לְמַלְאַךְ הַמָּוֶת,
דְּשָׁחַט לַשּׁוֹחֵט, דְּשָׁחַט לְתוֹרָא,
דְּשָׁתָה לְמַיָּא, דְּכָבָה לְנוּרָא,
דְּשָׂרַף לְחוּטְרָא, דְּהִכָּה לְכַלְבָּא,
דְּנָשַׁךְ לְשׁוּנְרָא, דְּאָכַל לְגַדְיָא,
דְּזַבֵּן אַבָּא בִּתְרֵי זוּזֵי;
חַד גַּדְיָא, חַד גַּדְיָא.

V'ata ha-kadosh baruch hu,
v'shachat l'mal-ach ha-mavet
d'shachat la-shochet, d'shachat l'tora,
d'shata l'maya, d'chava l'nura,
d'saraf l'chutra, d'hika l'chalba,
d'nashach l'shunra, d'achal l'gadya,
diz'van aba bitrei zuzei;
chad gadya, chad gadya.

*   *

p. 106

Chad gadya, chad gadya,
that father bought for two zuzim;
chad gadya, chad gadya.

Then came the cat and ate the kid
that father bought for two zuzim;
chad gadya, chad gadya.

Then came the dog and bit the cat that ate the kid
that father bought for two zuzim;
chad gadya, chad gadya.

Then came the stick and beat the dog
that bit the cat that ate the kid
that father bought for two zuzim;
chad gadya, chad gadya.

Then fire came and burnt the stick that beat the dog
that bit the cat that ate the kid
that father bought for two zuzim;
chad gadya, chad gadya.

Then water came and quenched the fire
that burnt the stick that beat the dog
that bit the cat that ate the kid
that father bought for two zuzim;
chad gadya, chad gadya.

Then came the ox and drank the water that quenched the fire
that burnt the stick that beat the dog
that bit the cat that ate the kid
that father bought for two zuzim;
chad gadya, chad gadya.

The butcher came and slew the ox
that drank the water that quenched the fire
that burnt the stick that beat the dog
that bit the cat that ate the kid
that father bought for two zuzim;
chad gadya, chad gadya.

Along came the angel of death
and slew the butcher that slew the ox
that drank the water that quenched the fire
that burnt the stick that beat the dog
that bit the cat that ate the kid
that father bought for two zuzim;
chad gadya, chad gadya.

Along came the
Holy One, the
One who is
blessed,
and slew the
angel of death
that slew the
butcher that
slew the ox
that drank the
water that
quenched the
fire
that burnt the
stick that beat
the dog
that bit the cat
that ate the kid
that father
bought for two
zuzim;
chad gadya,
chad gadya.

Candle Lighting

A. W. Binder

p. 4

Ba - ruch a -ta A-do-nai, E - lo - hei - nu me-lech ha-o - -
lam a - sher ki-d' sha - nu b'-mits-vo - tav v' tsi -
va - nu l' had-lik neir l' had-lik neir shel Yom Tov.
(on Shabbat) shel sha - bat v' shel Yom Tov.

Kiddush

Trad. Arr. by Kenneth B. Cohen

pp. 7–9

Ba - ruch a -ta A-do-nai, E - lo - hei - nu me-lech ha-o - lam, bo -
rei p' ri ha - ga - fen. Ba - ruch a-ta A-do-nai, E - lo -
hei - nu me - lech ha-o - lam, a - sher ba-char ba-nu mi-kol am, v' ro -
ma-ma-nu mi-kol la-shon, v' kid - sha-nu b'mitz-vo-tav. Va-ti - ten la-nu, A-do-nai E-lo-hei-nu b' a-ha-
va (shab-ba-tot lim-nu - cha) u' mo-a-dim l' sim-cha, cha-gim uz' ma-nim l' sa-
son, et yom (ha-sha-bat ha-zeh v' et yom) chag ha-ma-tzot ha-zeh z'

99

man·chei-ru-tei-nu, (b' a-ha-va) mik-ra ko — desh, zei-cher li-tsi-at Mits-ra — yim. Ki

va — — nu va-char — — ta v' o-ta — — nu Li-

dash — — ta mi — kol__ ha-a-mim, (v'shab-bat) u' mo-a-dei__ kod-sh' cha__ (b'

a-ha-va uv' ra-tson,)b'sim-cha uv' sa-son__ hin-chal-ta — — — nu. Ba-

ruch a-ta A-do-nai m' ka-deish (Ha-shab-bat v') Yis-ra — el
Yis-ra — el v' haz'ma-nim

ruch a-ta A-do-nai, E - lo - hei - nu me-lech ha-o-lam, she-he-che-ya-nu, v'

ki -y' ma — nu, v' hi - gi - ya - nu laz' - - - man ha - - zeh.

Ha Lachma

Learned from Pinchas Stern

Recited freely

Ha __ lach-ma an-ya di a - cha-lu a-va-ha-ta-na b' ar' a d' mitz-ra — yim.

kol dich-fin yei-tei v' yei - chul,__   Ha-sha-ta ha-cha,__ la-sha-na ha-ba'
kol dits-rich yei-tei v' yif - sach.__

a, b' ar' a d' yis-ra' el.   Ha-sha-ta av-dei, la-sha-na ha-ba' a __ b' nei cho-rin.__

Ma Nishtana

p. 14

Ma Nishtana

p. 14

Dayeinu

p. 39

101

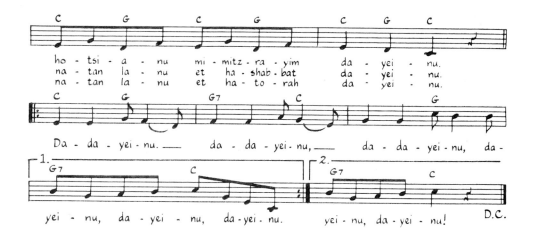

ho - tsi - a - nu mi - mitz - ra - yim da - yei - nu.
na - tan la - nu et ha - shab - bat da - yei - nu.
na - tan la - nu et ha - to - rah da - yei - nu.

Da - da - yei - nu.___ da - da - yei - nu,___ da - da - yei - nu, da -

1. yei - nu, da - yei - nu, da - yei - nu.
2. yei - nu, da - yei - nu!

D.C.

B'tzeit Yisrael

Triumphant march

Manistrisher Rebbe

B'tzeit yis - ra - eil mi - mitz-ra-yim beit ya - a - kov
Ma l' cha ha - yam ki ___ ta - nus? Ha - yar - dein

mei - am ___ lo - eiz ha - y'Lu y' hu - da l' ___ kod - sho,
ti - sov l' a - chor he ___ ha - rim tirk' du k' ei - lim?

yis - ra - eil yis - ra - eil mam-sh' lo - tav ha - yam ra - a ___
g' - va - ot g' - va - ot kiv' nei - tzon? mi - lif - nei a - don ___

ra - a v' ya - nos, ___ ha - yar dein yi - sov l' a - chor he - ha - rim
chu - li a - retz mi - lif-nei a-don E-loah ya - a - kov ha - hof' chi

rak - k' du ch' ei - lim, g' va - ot ___ kiv ___ nei - tzon.
ha - tsur a-gam ma - yim, cha - - - la - mish l' ma-no ma - yim.

Fine

p. 45

102

Eliyahu Hanavi

Softly with longing

Folk Song

p. 77

Ei - li-ya-hu ha-na-vi, Ei - li-ya-hu ha-tish-bi,

Ei - li-ya-hu Ei - li-ya-hu Ei - li-ya--hu ha-gil-a-di.

Fine

With optimism

bim-hei - ra b' ya-mei - nu ya - vo ei - lei - nu.
Im-ma-shi - ach ben Da-vid Im-ma-shi - ach ben Da-vid.

D.C. al Fine

Ki Lo Na-eh

With reverence

With a lilt

M. Nathanson

p. 83

Ki lo na-eh ki lo ya - eh. }
1. A - dir bim-lu - cha,
2. Da-gul bim-lu - cha,

March

ba-chur ka-ha-la-chah, ge - du-dav yom' ru lo, le - { cha u' le-cha le-
ha-dar ka-ha-la-chah, va - ti-kav yom' ru lo, le -

cha ki le - cha le - cha af le - cha, le - cha A - do-nai ha - mam-la-cha.

D.C.

Adir Hu

Majestically

J. S. Rittangels Haggadah - Germany

Repeat this bar as needed
in remaining verses.

pp. 86-88

1. A - dir hu, a - dir hu, yig - a - lei - nu b' ka - rov,
2. Awe-some One, awe-some One, soon may You re - deem us,
3. God of might, God of right, Rock of our sal - va - tion,

bim - hei - ra _____ bim - hei - ra b' ya - mei - nu b' ka - - rov.
speed - i - ly, _____ speed - i - ly, _____ soon with - in our life - time.
un - to You _____ still we do _____ of - fer A - dor - a - tion.

Eil p' dei, Eil p' dei, p' dei am' cha b' ka - rov
Save, O God; Save, O God, _____ Save Your peo-ple speed-i-ly.
Since Your hand from E - gypt's land _____ led Your joy-ful Na - tion.

D.C.

Echad Mi Yodea

Israeli

pp. 89, 91

Echad Mi Yodea

Oriental Community in Jerusalem

p. 89

Kareiv Yom

Chassidic Folk Song

p. 93

Ana Halach Dodeich

Shir Hashirim – Kenneth B. Cohen

p. 93

Let My People Go!

Kenneth B. Cohen

p. 94

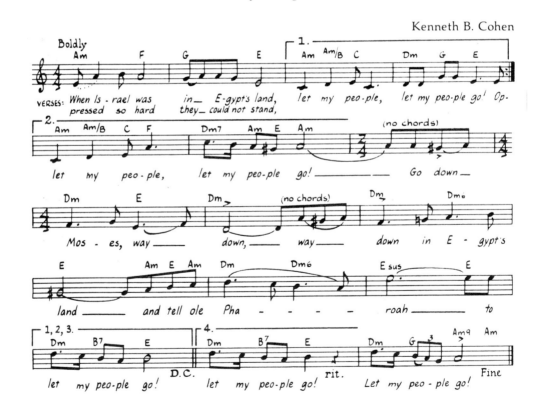

Let My People Go!

p. 94

Chad Gadya

pp. 95, 97

* After each new verse, repeat prior verses, then D.C.

Much of the music of the Seder comes from ancient and medieval sources. Throughout our history, Jewish composers have returned to cantillation as the earliest source of our musical tradition. A. W. Binder contends that biblical cantillation is the basis of our prayer modes, traditional melodies (i.e., *Kol Nidre*), folk songs, and art music. Biblical cantillation inspires us even today (see, e.g., *Ana Halach Dodeich*, based on the Ashkenazic cantillation for *Shir Hashirim*—Song of Songs). Examples of later influences upon the music of the Seder are found in the *Kiddush* (Germany, 11th–13th centuries) and *Adir Hu* (Germany, 17th century).

In every generation and locale, Jews have sought to relive the Exodus through the words of the Seder and through its music. For this music we have looked to the past, and have, in age after age, created new expressions to celebrate the miracle of freedom. May Israel's song ever be acceptable to God, who created us to be free.

Supplementary Readings

MINORITY RIGHTS

If all mankind minus one were of one opinion, and only one person were of the contrary opinion, mankind would be no more justified in silencing that one person, than he, if he had the power, would be justified in silencing mankind. (John Stuart Mill)

THE ONLY RIGHT USE OF POWER

The only purpose for which power can be rightfully exercised over any member of a civilised community, against his will, is to prevent harm to others. (John Stuart Mill)

FORMS OF OPPRESSION

The instinct of nearly all societies is to lock up anybody who is truly free. First, society begins by trying to beat you up. If this fails, they try to poison you. If this fails, too, they finish by loading honors on your head. (Jean Cocteau)

KNOW WHERE YOU ARE GOING

If you cry "forward!" you must without fail make plain in what direction to go. (Anton Chekhov)

REVOLUTION DEVOURS THE BEST

The scrupulous and the just, the noble, humane and devoted natures, the unselfish and the intelligent, may begin a movement—but it passes away from them. They are not the leaders of a revolution. They are its victims. (Joseph Conrad)

WHY LIBERTY?

Without liberty heavy industry can be perfected, but not justice or truth. (Albert Camus)

FOR FREEDOM TO BE REAL (I)

The freedom we should seek is not the right to oppress others, but the right to live as we choose and think as we choose where our doing so does not prevent others from doing likewise. (Bertrand Russell)

FOR FREEDOM TO BE REAL (II)

The only freedom that is of enduring importance is freedom of intelligence, that is to say, freedom of observation and of judgment exercised in behalf of purposes that are instrinsically worthwhile. (John Dewey)

FOR FREEDOM TO BE REAL (III)

Freedom from restriction . . . is to be prized only as a means to a freedom which is power: power to frame purposes, to judge wisely, to evaluate desires by the consequences which will result from acting upon them; power to select and order means to carry chosen ends into operation. (John Dewey)

FOR FREEDOM TO BE REAL (IV)

To say that a man is free to choose to walk while the only walk he can take will lead him over a precipice is to strain words as well as facts. (John Dewey)

FOR FREEDOM TO BE REAL (V)

Freedom is participation in power. (Marcus Tullius Cicero)

LOVE SICK

". . . for I am sick with love." (Song of Songs 2.5)
The congregation of Israel said to the Holy One: Ruler of the universe, all the ills You bring upon me are to make me love You the more. Another interpretation: The congregation of Israel said to the Holy One: Ruler of the universe, all the ills the nations of the world bring upon me are because I love You. (Midrash)

THE FOUR FREEDOMS

In the future days . . . we look forward to a world founded upon four essential freedoms.

The first is freedom of speech and expression. . . .
The second is freedom of every person to worship God in his own way. . . .
The third is freedom from want. . . .
The fourth is freedom from fear. . . .   (Franklin D. Roosevelt)

I believe there are more instances of the abridgement of the freedom of the people by gradual and silent encroachments of those in power than by violent and sudden usurpations. (James Madison)

SHABBAT: FREEDOM

There are higher objects in life than success. The Sabbath, with its exhortation to the worship of God and the doing of kindly deeds, reminds us week by week of these higher objects. It prevents us from reducing our life to the level of a machine. The Sabbath is one of the glories of our humanity. For if to labor is noble, of our own free will to pause in that labor which may lead to success, to money or to fame, may be nobler still. To dedicate one day a week to rest and to God, this is the prerogative and privilege of man alone. It is an ordinance we may rightly call divine. (Claude G. Montefiore)

HOW TO LOSE FREEDOM

In the end, more than they wanted freedom, they wanted security. When the Athenians finally wanted not to give to society but for society to give to them, when the freedom they wished for was freedom from responsibility, then Athens ceased to be free. (Edward Gibbon)

'FIT' TO BE FREE

Many politicians . . . are in the habit of laying it down as a self-evident proposition, that no people ought to be free until they are fit to use their freedom. The maxim is worthy of the fool . . . who resolved not to go into the water until he had learned to swim. (Thomas Babington Macaulay)

Notes

Abbreviations and Notations

Abrahams   Israel Abrahams, *A Companion to the Authorized Daily Prayerbook* (page references to Hermon Press edition, New York, 1966).

AMPH   *A Modern Passover Haggadah*, edited by John D. Rayner in collaboration with Chaim Stern and with the assistance of Rabbi Julia Neuberger, under the aegis of the Rabbinic Conference of the Union of Liberal and Progressive Synagogues (ULPS), (ULPS, London, 1981).

CS   Rabbi Chaim Stern (editor of this Haggadah; and see AMPH)

EJ   *Encyclopaedia Judaica* (Keter Publishing House, Ltd., Jerusalem, 1972)

Goldschmidt   E. D. Goldschmidt, *Haggadah shel Pesach V'toldoteha* (Bialik Institute, Jerusalem, 1969)

JDR   Rabbi John D. Rayner (principal editor of AMPH).

JE   *Jewish Encyclopedia* (Funk & Wagnalls Company, New York and London, 1907)

Kasher   Menachem M. Kasher, *Haggadah Shelemah* (Torah Shelemah Institute, Jerusalem, 1967)

Mishnah   Fundamental Rabbinic law-compilation completed in Palestine in the third century C.E.

MODERN   A passage appearing in a previous modern Haggadah, but not in the traditional Haggadah.

NEW   A passage newly written for the present Haggadah. It may also appear in AMPH, sometimes with changes.

NOVEL   A passage first utilized (so far as we know) in the present Haggadah. It may also appear in AMPH. Such a passage may be Biblical, Rabbinic, or contemporary.

NUH   *The New Union Haggadah*, edited by Rabbi Herbert Bronstein for the Central Conference of American Rabbis (CCAR, N.Y., 1974)

O.Ch.	*Orach Chayim* (Part I of the Arba-ah Turim, the fourteenth century law-code by Jacob ben Asher of Germany and Spain; like-wise of the Shulchan Aruch, the sixteenth century law-code by Joseph Caro of Palestine with glosses by Moses Isserles of Poland)
R.	Rabbi
SPJH	*Services and Prayers for Jewish Homes,* the prayerbook of the Liberal Jewish Synagogue (London) published in 1918. It contained the first British Liberal Haggadah. It was revised in 1955 and published by the ULPS. The ULPS published an entirely new Haggadah, edited by JDR, 1962, now replaced by AMPH.
SRA	*Seder Rav Amram,* the first Jewish prayerbook, compiled by Amram ben Sheshna, Gaon of Sura, Babylonia, about 860 C.E. (page references to E. D. Goldschmidt's edition, Mossad Harav Kook, Jerusalem, 1971)
Talmud	Refers either to the Babylonian Talmud, completed approximately in the sixth century C.E., or the Jerusalem (also called 'Palestinian') Talmud, completed in the fourth century C.E.
Tosafot	Super-commentaries on the Babylonian Talmud by Franco-German scholars of the twelfth and thirteenth centuries.
TRAD.	A passage appearing in the traditional Haggadah.
ULPS	Union of Liberal and Progressive Synagogues (London)

A General Note on Translation

PAGE xiii, AND OFTEN ELSEWHERE: The traditional benediction-formula (Baruch ata Adonai, Eloheinu melech ha-olam . . .) has always been a problem to translate. Our translation is: "We praise You, Eternal God, Ruler of time and space . . .", but the reader is warned that translations are many and varied. We shall here discuss three of the six Hebrew words that introduce the formula: Baruch, Adonai, and (ha-)olam.

The word 'Baruch' is a passive participle meaning 'blessed' or 'praised'. So translated it leads to awkward English, such as "Praised are You . . .". One attempt to solve the problem is to treat the second word (ata, 'You') as though it weren't there, so that we get "Blessed is..." We have chosen instead to mistranslate the Hebrew so as to produce a simple English declaration, "We praise . . .", recognizing that the verb is now active rather than passive, but feeling that it is the least bad Englishing of an infernally elusive Hebrew locution.

The word 'Adonai' is equally interesting. Usually it is translated as "Lord." It is an accurate translation for the word that, long ago, was introduced as a *substitute* for the pronouncing of the sacred Name of God, which is spelled (unvocalized) YHVH but pronounced ADONAI, from ADON, "LORD." "Lord" has the virtue, also, of being a word with four letters, and it is in that respect reminiscent of the four-letter Divine Name YHVH. There are, however, two objections that may be laid against the use of "Lord" for YHVH: it is masculine, and God has no gender and should not be spoken of in exclusively masculine terms; and it fails to convey to the English reader the root-meaning of YHVH, which is related to the verb for *being*. God (YHVH/Adonai) is the One-Who-Is-Was-Will Be. Therefore, we have chosen to render Adonai (and in this we follow the German usage) by "Eternal," and occasionally simply as Adonai.

The word 'ha-olam' is generally translated as "the world" or "the universe," and there is nothing wrong with either usage. It seemed to us, however, that we had an opportunity to convey something about an association inherent in Hebrew by a somewhat more adventurous translation, so for "olam" ("ha-" is merely the definite article) we give: "Time and space"—an expression for "universe" that has the advantage of reminding us that the word "olam" ('world,' 'universe') when prefixed by *l'* ('to'), means *forever*: hence, *time* and space. Thus we have come to the formula: "We praise You, Eternal God, Ruler of time and space . . ."

The benediction-formula we have been discussing has two forms, 'long' and 'short'. Both appear in the Haggadah. The long form contains the words 'asher kid'shanu b'mitzvotav', rendered by some as "who has sanctified (or, hallowed) us with His commandments." We prefer to remain in the second person, for stylistic reasons and in order to avoid using the masculine pronoun when referring to God. Moreover, the Hebrew "Mitzvot" (commandments) is rich and well-known; we retain it untranslated.

Thus the formula begins: "We praise You, Eternal God, Ruler of time and space" and continues: "for You hallow us with *Your* Mitzvot."

PAGE 14 (The Four Questions): The opening sentence is in fact an exclamation: "How different is this night from all other nights!" Because the less accurate "Why is this night different . . ." is so well-known and preferred, we have chosen to retain it.

PAGE 15 (THE FOUR CHILDREN): The 'children' are often called the "four sons." We have preferred to be more general, knowing that there are as many daughters as sons. Similarly, the introductory Hebrew is in the masculine singular; our English is plural: "The questions children ask." We believe we are being faithful to the intent of the Hebrew. It should be borne in mind that the Seder is a group ceremony, and the use of the plural, where the English is likely to be read, serves to include all the celebrants, and that is all to the good. This comment applies as well, and perhaps especially, to the passage on page 21 ("Arami oveid avi") literally, "My father was a wandering Aramean." In its original setting (Deuteronomy 26) it was a formula to be recited by *individuals* in a thanksgiving ceremony; here, in the Seder, its function is communal, and it seems right, therefore, to translate it into the plural.

In general, it seems to us that the occasional translation of Hebrew singulars as English plurals, and of third person to second, has a beneficial effect. Thus, for example, page 30: "You Yourself . . . in all Your glory" gains power from its direct address, and is to be preferred over the literal "He Himself . . . in all His glory."

This Note would not be complete without this demurrer: the foregoing should not mislead the reader into supposing that the Hebrew has not been faithfully translated. Almost always, it has not been necessary to make changes; and the few changes—noted above—are a faithful, if not always a literal, movement from Hebrew, a Semitic language, into English, very much non-Semitic in nature; and from texts written two or three thousand years ago into English that must mediate between past and present. No translation is the original. This translation proposes to reproduce the emotional reality behind the Hebrew. If we have caught something of its ethos, we are content.

113

Sources

7 *We praise . . . Festivals.* TRAD. Known as *Kiddush*, short for *Kiddush Hayom*, 'Sanctification of the Day,' this benediction is often referred to in Rabbinic Literature (Mishnah Pesachim 10.2; Babylonian Talmud: Pesachim 105a, Beitsah 17a), but the full text is first found in post-talmudic sources (Soferim 19.2; SRA, pp. 110 f.)

8 *We praise . . . fire.* TRAD., Mishnah Berachot 8.5. When the Sabbath is followed by a Festival, the custom is, not to light a special candle as when it is followed by an ordinary day, but merely to look at the already-kindled Festival lights when reciting this benediction (which is cited in Mishnah Berachot 8.5).

8 *We praise . . . holiness of Yom Tov.* TRAD., the principal benediction of the *Havdalah* ('Separation' or 'Distinction') ceremony according to the version used when the Sabbath is followed by a Festival. It is first cited in the Babylonian Talmud: Pesachim 103b.

9 *We praise . . . this season.* Known as *Shehecheyanu*, this is the benediction recited at the beginning of a Festival (and on other happy occasions). It is cited in various places in the Babylonian Talmud, including Pesachim 7b.

10 *Spring hangs . . .* The opening sentence, in quotation marks, is from a poem, *Tirocinium*, by William Cowper. The rest of the passage is adapted from a NEW passage by JDR in AMPH.

11 *Rise up, my love . . .* MODERN, Songs of Songs 2.11 f. Traditionally, the Song of Songs is read on the morning of the Sabbath in Pesach, though at one time it was read on the last two eves (see Soferim 14.18). There is also a custom to read it after the Seder; hence it is found at the end of some Haggadot. The quotation from it in the present context was an innovation of SPJH, and it is found in many modern Haggadot. The second stanza ('The standing corn . . .') is from *Tal*, the prayer for 'Dew,' traditionally inserted in the *Musaf* (Additional) service on the first day of Pesach. The present passage is an excerpt from a version of *Tal* that appears in the *Sefardi* liturgy. The translation, by CS, appeared first in GOP, p. 493, where it serves as an introductory prayer in the Pesach morning service. Its use here is an innovation of this Haggadah.

11 *The green herbs are dipped in salt water . . .* TRAD. The Mishnah (Pesachim 10.3) says that *Chazeret*, lettuce, is to be dipped, but does not make it clear in what. The custom of using *Karpas*, parsley, and of dipping it in salt water (or vinegar), symbolic of the tears shed by the Israelite slaves in Egypt (and, secondarily, of the ocean in which life was born), is first mentioned in medieval sources

115

(Tosafot to Babylonian Talmud, Pesachim 114a; Shulchan Aruch, O.Ch. 473.4; see Kasher, pp. 101–106).

11 *We praise . . . earth.* TRAD. The benediction to be recited, according to the Mishnah (Berachot 6.1), before eating any fruit or vegetable grown on the ground.

12 *God is bread . . .* NOVEL. A saying of Mohandas K. Gandhi.

12 *The leader takes out . . .* The plain reason for the three Matzot is that the top and bottom ones correspond to the two loaves of bread customary on the eve of the Sabbath or a Festival (in allusion, it is said, to the double portion of Manna granted the Israelites for the Sabbath in their wandering throught the wilderness, Exod. 16.22), while the middle one represents the 'bread of affliction' (Deut. 16.3). Medieval sources also give fanciful explanations, e.g., that the three Matzot refer to the Three Patriarchs (Abraham, Isaac, and Jacob), or the three measures of flour with which Sarah baked bread for the three angelic visitors (Genesis 18.6), or the three classes of Israelites (Priest, Levite, Israelite) into which the people were divided in ancient times. See Kasher, pp. 61 f.

12 *This is the bread of affliction . . .* TRAD. An Aramaic formula first found, in various forms, in Gaonic Rites (SEE SRA, p. 113; Kasher, pp. 106–12; Goldschmidt, pp. 7 ff.). The first sentence alludes to Deut. 16.3; the second is based on an invitation to the poor to share one's meal found already in the Babylonian Talmud, Ta'anit 20b.

13 *Should I celebrate . . .* MODERN. A new translation, by CS, of a poem entitled '1959, Russia' by Samuel Halkin (1897–1960), a Soviet Yiddish writer who suffered exile in Siberia. The poem is included in NUH, pp. 46 ff., with another translation.

14 *Why is this night different . . .* TRAD. First found in the Mishnah (Pesachim 10.4), but with *three* and somewhat different questions. By Gaonic times there was substantial modification and by SRA, p. 113, we have the text as now. See Kasher, pp. 112–17; Goldschmidt, pp. 10–13.

14 *You are free . . .* NEW, by CS.

15 *The questions children ask . . .* NOVEL, from the Mechilta d'R. Shimon ben Yochai to Exod. 13.14. Also in AMPH.

15 *And parents should . . .* NOVEL, from the Mishnah, Pesachim 10.4. Also in AMPH.

16 *The Torah alludes . . .* TRAD. First found, in divergent versions, in Rabbinic Literature (Mechilta to Exod. 13.14 and the Jerusalem (Palestinian) Talmud, Pesachim 10.4) and, further modified, in the

Gaonic Rites (See SRA, p. 114; Kasher, pp. 120–23; Goldschmidt, pp. 22–29). The wise child is derived from Deut. 6.20 and Mishnah Pesachim 10.8; the wicked child from Exodus 12.26 and 13.8; the simple one from Exod. 13.14; and the one who does not know enough to ask from Exod. 13.8.

17 *Suffering and love* . . . MODERN. A widely-told Chasidic tale. Levi Yitzchak of Berditchev (c. 1740–1809) was a leading Chasidic Rebbe noted for his compassionate love of Israel, which led him to call God to account for Jewish suffering. See M. Buber, *Tales of the Hasidim,* Vol. 1, pp. 212f. Also in NUH.

17 *The wicked child* . . . NOVEL. Babylonian Talmud, Ta'anit 11a.

17 *The basic freedom* . . . NOVEL. By George Orwell, in *1984,* VII.

18 *Our story begins* . . . NOVEL, from Mishnah Pesachim 10.4. Also in AMPH.

18 *We were slaves* . . . TRAD., mentioned in the Babylonian Talmud, Pesachim 116a, which says that the Third Century teacher Samuel advocated the recitation of this passage as fulfilling the principle to 'begin with degradation and end with glory' (See preceding Note). The full text is first found in Gaonic Rites (See SRA, pp. 113 f.; Kasher, pp. 117–20).

18 *They say* . . . TRAD. This Midrash is first found in Gaonic Rites (See SRA, p. 114). The five rabbis mentioned lived in Palestine in the first-second centuries. B'nei B'rak was a place near Jaffa. It has been conjectured that the event described here took place just before the Bar Kochba revolt against Roman rule (132–35 C.E.), and that the rabbis were actually planning the revolt. That may or may not be. The Tosefta, a source parallel to the Mishnah, contains a similar story (See Tosefta, Pesachim 10.12), but with other characters, and taking place in Lydda, not B'nei B'rak.

19 *Rabbi Elazar ben Azariah* . . . TRAD., from Mishnah Berachot 1.5. Our translation is not literal.

19 *Our story begins* . . . TRAD. First mentioned in the Babylonian Talmud, Pesachim 116a, as the passage favored by the Third Century teacher Rav as fulfilling the principle to 'begin with degradation and end with glory,' as against his colleague Samuel, who favored the passage 'We were slaves' (See above, last Note but three). The full text is first found in Gaonic Rites (See SRA, p. 114; Kasher, pp. 27 ff.). The quotation is Joshua 24.2 ff.

20 *Our story begins* . . . NOVEL, from Mishnah Pesachim 10.4. Also in AMPH.

20 *Our ancestors* . . . TRAD., Deuteronomy 26.5–8. Mentioned already in the Mishnah, Pesachim 10.4, as the basis of the exposition which forms the bulk of the Haggadah-narrative. The translation here, as occasionally elsewhere in this Haggadah, departs from the literal in order to avoid liturgically unnecessary masculine language. The Hebrew is written in the singular ('My father was a wandering Aramean . . . '), meaning 'forefather,' and referring to Abraham, Jacob, or the Patriarchs collectively. The Editor prefers 'ancestors,' so that our 'foremothers' may be included by us in our collective memory.

21 *We began as wanderers* . . . NEW, by CS. Also in AMPH.

21 *Though upon our arrival* . . . NEW, by CS, alluding to Exodus 6.9. Also (with slight differences) in AMPH.

21 *The habit of bondage* . . . NOVEL. By George Gordon, Lord Byron, *The Prisoner of Chillon,* XIV. Also in AMPH.

21 *The real slavery* . . . NOVEL. A saying of R. Hanokh of Aleksandrow (1798–1870, Poland), quoted by Martin Buber in *Tales of the Hasidim,* Vol. 2, p. 315. Also in AMPH.

21 *Who has not made me a slave* . . . NOVEL. A responsum by Rabbi Ephraim Oshry to a question asked by a fellow-concentration camp inmate, in *She-eilot U-t'shuvot Mima'amakim* ("Questions and Answers from the Depths").

22 *Our ancestors* . . . TRAD., Deuteronomy 10.22. First found in SRA, p. 114. This translation renders a second person singular into first person plural.

22 *The use of the word* . . . The first sentence is TRAD., and refers to a passage from the Mechilta to Exodus 12.6, first used verbatim in NUH, p. 38, and also in AMPH. Here, however, it serves to introduce a passage from the Babylonian Talmud, Yevamot 79a, whose use here is NOVEL.

23 *The people* . . . TRAD., Exodus 1.17. First found in SRA, p. 114.

23 *As it is said* . . . TRAD., Exodus 1.8–10. First found in SRA, p. 114.

23 *Shifrah and Puah* . . . NOVEL. Two passages from the Midrash, Exodus Rabbah 1.14, 1.15, quoting Exodus 1.17.

25 *To struggle for freedom* . . . NOVEL. By Frederick Douglass.

25 *As it is said . . . Raamses.* TRAD., Exodus 1.11. First found in SRA, p. 114.

26 *As it is said . . . themselves.* TRAD., Exodus 1.13. First found in SRA, p. 114. The remainder of the passage is NOVEL, from the Midrash, Exodus Rabbah 5.18.

27   *As it is said . . . God.* TRAD., Exodus 2.23. First found in SRA, p. 114.

27   *As it is said . . . covenant.* TRAD., Exodus 2.24. First found in SRA, p. 114.

27   *And that covenant . . .* NEW, by CS.

28   *We have learned . . .* NOVEL, from the Midrash.

28   *It is said . . . God knew.* TRAD., Exodus 2.25.

28   *God saw . . . wives.* TRAD. First found in SRA, p. 114. It is based on a legend found in the Babylonian Talmud (Sotah 74b) that the Egyptians forbade the Israelites to procreate. The preceding passage (Exodus 2.25) is the prooftext for this observation, though the connection between them is not clear.

28   *It is said . . . Nile.* TRAD., Exodus 1.22. First found in SRA, p. 114. This becomes the prooftext for the next passage.

28   *God saw . . . children.* TRAD. First found in SRA, p. 114. In the trad. Haggadah, this passage *precedes* the previous one.

28   *And it is said . . . oppress them.* NOVEL, Exodus 3.9. Also in AMPH.

28   *God saw . . . our spirit.* NEW, by CS.

29   *God said: "How well I see . . .* NOVEL, Exodus 3.7. Also in AMPH.

29   *Our plight . . .* NEW, by CS, introducing two NOVEL passages (both of which are also in AMPH): Judges 10.16 (here slightly adapted) and Isaiah 63.9. 21.

29   *And we have learned . . .* NOVEL, from the Babylonian Talmud, Megillah 29a. Also in AMPH.

29   *The 'wage slave' . . .* NOVEL. From a passage by John Ruskin, in *Fors Clavigera*, letter 46.

30   *The benevolent despot . . .* NOVEL. From a passage by Leo Tolstoy.

30   *Power over women . . .* NOVEL. By John Stuart Mill, in *Subjugation of Women*, II.

30   *Not by an angel . . .* TRAD. First found in SRA, p. 114, but based on a passage in the Jerusalem (Palestinian) Talmud, Sanhedrin 2.1 and Horayot 3.1.

31   *The Divine Presence . . .* TRAD. First found in SRA, p. 114, quoting Deuteronomy 4.34.

31   *No liberation is easy . . .* NEW, by JDR and CS. Also (with some minor differences) in AMPH.

31 *Apathy in the face of evil* . . . NEW, by CS. An acrostic, with the first ten letters of the English alphabet, of evils, ancient and modern, to introduce the Ten Plagues.

31 *We look back now* . . . NEW, by CS.

31 *A drop of wine* . . . TRAD. The custom is mentioned in medieval sources (see Shulchan Aruch, O.Ch., gloss; Kasher, p. 125 f.). Our interpretation of it is based on that of Don Isaac Abravanel (1437–1508), who related it to the injunction, "Do not rejoice when your enemy falls," (Proverbs 24.17). For the Ten Plagues, see Exodus 7.14–12.36.

34 *To choose* . . . NOVEL, from a passage by Victor Frankl, in *Man's Search for Meaning*, p. 65.

34 *When the cup of suffering* . . . NEW, by CS. Also in AMPH.

34 *At that time, when Israel stood* . . . NOVEL, from the Midrash, Mechilta to Exodus 14.22. Nachshon was a chieftain of the tribe of Judah; see Numbers 2.3, 10.14. Also in AMPH.

35 *At that time, they plunged* . . . NOVEL, from the Midrash, Exodus Rabbah 21.10. Also in AMPH, in abridged form.

35 *The people overcame* . . . NEW, by CS. Also (with substantial differences) in AMPH.

35 *Have no fear* . . . NOVEL, Isaiah 43.1 f. Also in AMPH.

35 *It is said: "When Israel saw* . . . The Biblical passage (Exodus 14.31) referring to the crossing of the Sea of Reeds (or Red Sea), is NOVEL (also in AMPH). The passage following, about the ministering angels, is from the Babylonian Talmud, Megillah 10b. It is MODERN, first used in the 1962 edition of the ULPS Haggadah, p. 10, and used subsequently in many Haggadot.

36 *O God, teach us* . . . NEW, by CS. Also in AMPH.

36 *That day is not yet* . . . NEW, by JDR. Also (with a slight difference) in AMPH.

36 *Fear not* . . . NOVEL, Isaiah 41.10. Also in AMPH.

36 *Blessed is the One* . . . TRAD., first found in SRA, p. 114. The traditional text goes on to quote Genesis 15.13 f.

37 *In each generation* . . . TRAD. First found in the Mishnah, Pesachim 10.5. The quotation is Exodus 13.8.

37 *For the Holy One* . . . TRAD., a continuation of the preceding, but first found in SRA, p. 114. The quotation is Deuteronomy 6.23.

37 *The slaveholder is not free* . . . NOVEL. By Ralph Waldo Emerson, in *Compensation*.

37 *The price of injustice* . . . NOVEL. By Henry David Thoreau.

37 *Do not become the enemy* . . . NOVEL. By Friedrich Nietzsche.

39 *How many gifts* . . . TRAD. & MODERN. The traditional text, which concludes with the building of the Temple, is first found in SRA, p. 115. In our version it is abridged but supplemented with five new verses, relating to the Prophets and post-biblical times. Similar attempts to bring this composition 'up to date' are to be found in the 1962 version of the ULPS Haggadah and in NUH. Also in AMPH.

41 *Therefore we thank* . . . TRAD., first found in the Mishnah, Pesachim 10.5.

42 *The courage to be free (I)* . . . NOVEL. From a passage by Mark Twain, in *Pudd'nhead Wilson's New Calendar*, XX.

42 *The courage to be free (II)* . . . NOVEL. From the Babylonian Talmud, Kiddushin 22b. The quotation is from Leviticus 25.55.

42 *The courage to be free (III)* . . . NOVEL. From the Midrash, Songs of Songs, Rabbah 4.2.

44 *Halleluyah* . . . TRAD. The custom of reciting the Hallel ('Praise') Psalms (113–18) during the Seder is mentioned already in the Mishnah, Pesachim 10.6f.

45 *When Israel went forth* . . . TRAD., Psalm 114. See preceding Note.

46 *We raise our cups* . . . MODERN. See the Note to the drinking of the First Cup, p. 6.

47 *We praise You . . . Redeemer of Israel*. TRAD., known as *G'ulah*, 'Redemption,' first cited in the Mishnah, Pesachim 10.6. Our version is slightly abridged, omitting a phrase about the hoped-for restoration of the sacrificial cult.

47 *We praise . . . vine*. TRAD. See corresponding Note to the wine benediction on p. 7.

48 *Rabban Gamaliel* . . . TRAD., already in the Mishnah, Pesachim 10.5. The reference is to Rabban Gamaliel I, grandson of Hillel. Gamaliel was Patriarch of Palestinian Jewry before the destruction of the Temple by the Romans in 70 C.E.

48 *Pesach: Why did our ancestors eat* . . . TRAD. Alluded to in the Mishnah, Pesachim 10.5. The full text is first found in SRA, p. 115, quoting Exodus 12.27.

48   *When the Temple still stood* . . . NEW, by CS and JDR. Also in AMPH, in slightly different form.

49   *This egg* . . . NEW, by JDR and CS. Also in AMPH.

49   *Matzah: Why do we eat it* . . . TRAD. Alluded to in the Mishnah, Pesachim 10.5. The full text is first found in SRA, p. 115, quoting Exodus 12.39.

49   *Free Romans* . . . NEW, by CS and JDR. Also in AMPH, in rather different from, by JDR and CS. The custom of 'leaning' or 'reclining' is mentioned already in the Mishnah, Pesachim 10.1. The Jerusalem (Palestinian) Talmud comments: "To show that they had come forth from slavery to freedom" (Pesachim 10.1). Medieval sources record various opinions on this custom, discussing who should lean, and whether to lean at all (Shulchan Aruch, O.Ch. 472.2–7; Kasher, p. 68–76).

50   *We praise . . . from the earth.* TRAD., the benediction to be recited before eating bread, as ordained in the Mishnah, Berachot 6.1. It alludes to Psalm 104.14.

50   *We praise . . . unleavened bread.* TRAD., first found, in a slightly different version, in SRA, p. 117.

50   *Maror: Why do we eat it* . . . TRAD. Alluded to in the Mishnah, Pesachim 10.5. First found in full in SRA, p. 115, quoting Exodus 1.14

50   *Before eating the Maror* . . . NEW, by JDR, in AMPH. Here adapted by CS. Further on the Charoset, see Shulchan Aruch, O.Ch. 473.5 and Kasher, pp. 62–4.

51   *We praise . . . bitter herbs.* TRAD., first found, with slightly different wording, in SRA, p. 116.

51   *This was Hillel's practice* . . . TRAD., quoting Numbers 9.11. The Tosefta (Pesachim 2.14) and Babylonian Talmud (Pesachim 115a) allude to it; the Gaonic and subsequent Rites have the full text in various versions (see SRA, p. 117; Kasher, pp. 169 ff.). Hillel was the leading Pharisaic teacher in Palestine in the last decades of the first century B.C.E.

51   *We hold* . . . NEW, by CS.

52   *This Matzah is called* . . . NEW, by CS and JDR, quoting Psalm 31.10. Also in AMPH. The Mishnah (Pesachim 10.8) makes a mysterious statement which, in our Haggadah, is translated: "We conclude the Pesach meal with Afikoman." It is the answer given to the Wise Child. It could just as well have been translated: "We

do *not* conclude the Pesach meal with Afikoman." The Babylonian Talmud (Pesachim 119b) records a debate between the third century teachers Rav and Samuel on the meaning of this passage of the Mishnah. Rav takes it to mean that we are not to go 'from company to company,' i.e., from one Seder to another; Samuel holds it to be a prohibition against a 'savory' or 'dessert' at the end of the Seder (for that would tend to take away the lingering flavor of the symbolic dishes, especially the Matzah). In 1925, Robert Eisler suggested that 'Afikoman' comes from the Greek *aphiko-menos*, meaning 'the one who comes,' i.e., the Messiah. This suggestion was subsequently revived by Professor David Daube in 1966, in a lecture later published in a pamphlet.

54   *A Song of Ascents* . . . TRAD. The custom of chanting Psalm 126 before the Thanksgiving for the Meal on Sabbaths and Festivals has been traced back to the year 1603 (Abrahams, p. 208).

54   *Let us praise God* . . . TRAD. This and the following introductory formulae are cited already in the Mishnah (Berachot 7.3) and Talmuds (Jerusalem Berachot 7.2; Babylonian Berachot 45a-b, 49b-50a).

54   *We praise . . . who live.* TRAD., the first of the four benedictions constituting *Birkat Hamazon*, the 'Thanksgiving for Food.' Derived from Deuteronomy 8.10, this institution is mentioned already in Josephus (*Wars of the Jews*, II, 8.5). The text is first cited in the Babylonian Talmud (Berachot 48b).

55   *Eternal our God . . . for the land and for the food.* TRAD., the second of the four benedictions. The quotation is Deuteronomy 8.10. For the traditional 'the covenant You have sealed into our flesh' we have substituted' . . . into our hearts' (cf. Deuteronomy 10.16 and 30.6), so that the phrase may be appropriately recited by men and women alike. Also in AMPH.

55   *O God, Source of our being . . . will build Jerusalem. Amen.* TRAD., the third of the four benedictions, slightly abridged. In the interpolation for the Sabbath we have substituted 'the consolation of Your people and the building of Your City' for 'the consolation of Your city Zion and the rebuilding of Your holy city Jerusalem,' in order to make explicit the broader, symbolic meaning implicit (not to the *exclusion* of the narrower, literal meaning) in these references to Zion and Jerusalem, and to suggest that the last two sentences of the benediction should be so understood.

56   *We praise . . . bless Your people with peace. Amen.* TRAD. This benediction, the last of the four, lacks a concluding eulogy. We

provide an abridged version. According to the Talmuds (Jerusalem Ta'anit 4.5; Babylonian Berachot 48b, Ta'anit 31a) it was introduced after the Bar Kochba rebellion of 132-135 C.E.; but many sentences, especially those beginning 'Merciful One . . . ,' were inserted much later, in the Middle Ages and subsequently (see Abrahams, pp. 209 f.). The text includes allusions to Proverbs 3.4 and Job 25.2, and ends with Psalm 29.11.

58 *A Song of Ascents* . . . TRAD. See first Note to p. 54.

59 *We praise . . . who live.* TRAD. See third Note to page 54.

62 *Merciful One . . . with peace. Amen.* These are excerpts from the fourth benediction, ending with Psalm 29.11. See Note to p. 56.

62 *We raise our cups* . . . MODERN. See the Note to the drinking of the first cup, p. 6.

63 *We praise . . . vine.* TRAD. See corresponding Note to the wine benediction on p. 7.

64 *Praise* . . . TRAD. Here the recitation of Hallel (see Note to p. 44) is resumed, traditionally, with Psalms 115-18. We, however, omit Psalms 115 and 116, for it is customary to omit these Psalms on the last six days of Pesach, one reason being that, on account of the drowning of the Egyptians in the Red Sea, we should restrain our rejoicing on the principle of 'Do not rejoice when your enemy falls' (Proverbs 24.17; Midrash, Pesikta d'R. Kahana, ed. Mandelbaum, II, 458). It seems to us appropriate to apply that principle in the Seder also. Following this reasoning, AMPH also omits these Psalms.

68 *Let all creation praise You* . . . TRAD. This doxology, which 'rounds off' the Hallel, is mentioned in the Babylonian Talmud (Pesachim 118a), where Rav Judah (Third Century teacher) identifies it with the 'Benediction of Song' which, according to the Mishnah (Pesachim 10.7) should be recited over the fourth cup of wine.

68 *Let every living soul* . . . TRAD. According to the Babylonian Talmud (Pesachim 118a), R. Yochanan (third century Palestinian teacher) identified it with the 'Benediction of Song' (*contra* Rav Judah—see preceding Note).

70 *'Fit' to be free* . . . NOVEL. By John Stuart Mill, in *Representative Government*, I.

71 *The Cup of Elijah* . . . The traditional Haggadah mandates, at this point, the drinking of the fourth cup of wine. We prefer to interpolate 'the Cup of Elijah,' although it is the 'fifth cup' (see the next Note).

71 *The cups are re-filled* . . . TRAD. The Babylonian Talmud (Pesachim 118a) records the view of R. Tarfon (first-second century Palestinian teacher) that there should be a *fifth* cup at the Seder; its derivation from the fifth verb of the Exodus 6.6–8 passage (one of the sources of the *four*-cup custom—see Notes to p. 6) is first found in twelfth century sources (see Kasher, p. 94 f.). Some Medieval Jewish authorities (e.g., Maimonides) considered the custom commendable but optional; others, like Abraham ben David of Posquieres, considered it obligatory (*ibid.*). The designation of the fifth cup as the 'Cup of Elijah' is first found in a commentary (Chok Yaakov) by Jacob Reischer (1670–1733, Bohemia) on the Shulchan Aruch (O.Ch. 480, Note 6).

71 *The door is opened* . . . TRAD. This custom originated in the Middle Ages and was widely practiced by the sixteenth century (see Kasher, p. 180). It was both a precaution against informers (to show there was nothing to hide, in view of the 'blood accusation') and an expression of trust in God's protection and of hope for the speedy coming of the messianic age, heralded by the return of the prophet Elijah. Traditionally, a passage beginning 'Pour out Your wrath . . .' (Psalms 79.6 f., 69.25 and Lamentations 3.66) is recited; of this, we retain only Psalm 79.7, as part of the new ritual in this Haggadah.

71 *Why do we drink* . . . NOVEL. See first Note to p. 6.

71 *I am Adonai* . . . Exodus 6.6 f. See second Note to p. 6.

72 *But there is a fifth promise* . . . NEW, by CS, quoting Exodus 6.8. Cf. the corresponding passage in AMPH.

72 *The world is far* . . . NEW, by CS.

72 *In every generation* . . . TRAD., part of a longer passage that appears earlier in the Haggadah. See Note to 'Blessed is the One' on p. 36.

73 *But the Holy One* . . . TRAD., a continuation of the preceding passage.

73 *We remember expulsions . . . to ash.* NEW, by CS.

73 *They have devoured* . . . TRAD., Psalm 79.7. See Note to 'The door is opened' on p. 71.

73 *But we have saved* . . . NEW, by CS. A variation on the passage cited in the last Note but two.

73 *For from these fugitives* . . . NEW, by CS.

73 *We shall remember* . . . NEW, by CS. The last sentence is TRAD., from the passage beginning 'We were slaves' on p. 18.

74 *We remember many glories* . . . NEW, by CS.

74 *Zion heard* . . . NOVEL. Psalm 97.8.

74 *But the full glory* . . . NEW, by CS and JDR.

75 *I will lift up the cup* . . . NOVEL. Psalm 116.13.

75 *Again, and yet again* . . . *our redemption shall begin. As it is written.* NEW, by CS, with allusions to I Kings 21 and 19.

76 *Behold, I am sending* . . . MODERN. Malachi 3.23 f. Also in AMPH. NUH, p. 70.

77 *And on that day* . . . *Land of Promise.* NEW, by CS, quoting Exodus 6.8.

77 *Eiliyahu hanavi* . . . MODERN. A traditional folk song that has become associated with Pesach, on account of its connection with the figure of Elijah and the theme of redemption.

78 *Today* . . . NOVEL, from the Babylonian Talmud, Sanhedrin 98a, quoting Psalm 95.7. R. Joshua ben Levi was a third century Palestinian teacher; R. Shimon bar Yochai was a second-century Palestinian teacher who was at one time condemned to death by the Romans and for some years took refuge in a cave.

79 *Our celebration* . . . NEW, by CS. This introduces a series of Biblical verses on the theme of remembrance of our servitude in Egypt, and of the ethical lesson to be drawn therefrom. A somewhat similar reading appears in *The New Haggadah* (Reconstructionist), Berhman House, Inc., N. Y., 1942, 1978. There it follows the Ten Plagues.

79 *As you rejoice* . . . *land of Egypt.* NOVEL. *Deuteronomy 16.11 f.*

79 *May our remembering* . . . NEW, by CS. An introduction to the next passage.

79 *The strangers in your midst* . . . MODERN, Leviticus 19.34. Also in *The New Haggadah*, p. 54.

79 *There shall be* . . . NEW, by CS. An introduction to the next passage.

79 *Only Me shall the people* . . . MODERN, Leviticus 25.55. Also in *The New Haggadah*, p. 56.

80 *Our redemption* . . . NEW, by CS. An introduction to the drinking of the fourth cup. On the quotation ("I will TAKE YOU . . .") see the Note to the drinking of the First Cup, p. 6.

81 *We praise* . . . *vine.* TRAD. See corresponding Note to the wine benediction on p. 7.

81 *We praise* . . . *to be free.* MODERN. This is one of a series of benedictions found in the morning service, first found in the Babylonian Talmud, Berachot 60b. There, however, the present

126

benediction is in the negative, 'who has not made me a slave.' The American Reform and Conservative liturgies both utilize the positive formulation, as does the (Conservative) Rabbinic Assembly's new "preliminary edition" of the Haggadah.

81 *Our Seder now concludes* . . . TRAD. and NEW. The Hebrew is the first stanza of a *piyyut* (liturgical poem) by Joseph ben Samuel Bonfils (eleventh century, France). The last four (English) lines are NEW, by CS.

81 *Tommorrow's promised Passover* . . . NEW, by CS (see preceding Note, end). Cf. the rabbinic thought (Babylonian Talmud, Rosh Hashanah 11b) that, as Israel was redeemed in the month of Nisan, so in that month *will* they be redeemed.

82 *Then all shall sit* . . . NOVEL. Micah 4.4. Also in AMPH.

82 *For us and all Israel* . . . NEW and TRAD. The first two lines, and the fourth are NEW, by CS, intended to make explicit the broader, universal hope, over and above the narrower, national one, that has always been implicit in the exclamation of the third line, "Next year in Jerusalem!" That line is traditionally recited immediately after the *piyyut* (see last Note but one), probably prompted by the conclusion of its second stanza (here omitted), "Soon may You lead the offshoots of Your planting, redeemed, to Zion in joy."

85 *To You praise belongs* . . . TRAD. A *piyyut* (liturgical poem) of unknown authorship that has been traced back to German, Italian, and English Haggadot of the thirteenth century (see Kasher, p. 189, Goldschmidt, p. 97), with an alphabetic acrostic, which the new translation (by JDR, here slightly adapted by CS) attempts to reproduce in English. Also in AMPH.

87 *Awesome One* . . . TRAD. A *piyyut* (liturgical poem) of unknown authorship which first appeared in Haggadot of the fourteenth century (see Kasher, p. 190, Goldschmidt, p. 97) with an alphabetic acrostic which the new translation (by JDR, here substantially revised by CS) attempts to reproduce in English. We have changed the phrase *yivneh veito b'karov*, "soon may He rebuild His Temple," to *yig-aleinu b'karov*, rendered here as "soon may You redeem us," and the refrain *b'nei beit'cha b'karov*, "rebuild Your Temple speedily," to *p'dei am'cha b'karov*, "save Your people speedily." Also in AMPH.

88 *God of might* . . . MODERN. A poem by Rabbi Gustav Gottheil (1827–1903, Germany, England, and U. S. A.), used in many Reform/Liberal Haggadot. This version goes back to the 1955 edition of SPJH. The first line of the third stanza is new, by CS.

91 *Who knows one* . . . TRAD. A composition of unknown authorship that has been traced back to the fifteenth century and was probably modelled on earlier, non-Jewish prototypes (see Kasher, p. 190, Goldschmidt, p. 98).

93 *Bring near the day* ('Kareiv Yom') . . . TRAD. The last stanza of a *piyyut* (liturgical poem) by Yannai, who probably lived in Palestine in the sixth or seventh century. Its inclusion in the Haggadah dates from about the twelfth century (see Kasher, p. 188, Goldschmidt, p. 96).

93 *Where has your love gone* ('Ana Halach Dodeich') . . . NOVEL. Song of Songs 6.1f. Included here, like the next two songs, because the Songs of Songs is traditionally read during Pesach (see Note to p. 11). Also in AMPH.

94 *My beloved is mine* ('Dodi Li') . . . NOVEL. Song of Songs 6.3, 4.9, 3.6, 4.16. Also in AMPH.

94 *I went down to the grove* ('El Ginat Egoz') . . . NOVEL. Song of Songs 6.11, 7.12f., 4.16. Also in AMPH.

94 *Let my people go* . . . MODERN. This North American Negro spiritual is found in a number of modern Haggadot. Also in AMPH.

97 *Chad Gadya* . . . TRAD. A composition of unknown authorship in somewhat impure Aramaic that has been traced back to the fifteenth century but was probably modelled on earlier, German prototypes (see Kasher, pp. 109f., Goldschmidt, p. 98). Its theme is paralleled by a number of passages in Rabbinic Literature—Mishnah Avot 2.6; Midrash, Genesis Rabbah 38.13; Babylonian Talmud, Bava Batra 10a.

107 *Minority rights* . . . NOVEL. From a passage by John Stuart Mill, in *On Liberty*, II.

107 *The only right use of power* . . . NOVEL. By John Stuart Mill.

107 *Forms of oppression* . . . NOVEL. By Jean Cocteau, quoted in *Time*, Sept. 30, 1957.

107 *Know where you are going* . . . NOVEL. By Anton Chekhov.

107 *Revolution devours the best* . . . NOVEL. BY Joseph Conrad.

107 *Why liberty* . . . NOVEL. By Albert Camus, in *Resistance, Rebellion and Death*.

107 *For freedom to be real (I)* . . . NOVEL. By Bertrand Russell, in *Sceptical Essays*, XIII.

108 *For freedom to be real (II)* . . . NOVEL. By John Dewey, in *Experience and Education*, V.

108 *For freedom to be real (III)* . . . NOVEL. By John Dewey, *Ibid.*

108 *For freedom to be real (IV)* . . . NOVEL. By John Dewey, in *Human Nature and Conduct*, IV, 3.

108 *For freedom to be real (V)* . . . NOVEL. By Marcus Tullius Cicero, in *Letter to Atticus.*

108 *Love-sick* . . . NOVEL. Midrash, Song of Songs Rabbah 2.14, quoting Song of Songs 2.5.

108 *The four freedoms* . . . NOVEL. From a speech by Franklin D. Roosevelt, *Message to Congress,* Jan. 6, 1941.

109 *Freedom may be lost* . . . NOVEL. By James Madison, in a Speech to the Virginia Convention, June 6, 1788.

109 *Shabbat: Freedom* . . . NOVEL, from a passage by Claude G. Montefiore.

109 *How to lose freedom* . . . NOVEL. By Edward Gibbon, in *Decline and Fall of the Roman Empire.*

109 *'Fit' to be free* . . . NOVEL. By Thomas Babington Macauley.